THE
Upside-Down
CHRISTMAS
TREE

And Other Bizarre Yuletide Tales

DELILAH SCOTT
and
EMMA TROY

Lyons Press
Guilford, Connecticut

An Imprint of Globe Pequot Press

Lyons Press is an imprint of Globe Pequot Press.

Text designed by Sheryl P. Kober
Layout by Melissa Evarts
Spot art © Shutterstock

Library of Congress Cataloging-in-Publication Data

Scott, Delilah.
  The upside-down christmas tree : and other bizarre yuletide tales /
Delilah Scott and Emma Troy.
      p. cm.
  Includes bibliographical references and index.
  ISBN 978-1-59921-419-1 (alk. paper)
  1. Christmas—Psychological aspects. 2. Christmas—Anecdotes. 3. Holiday stress. I. Troy, Emma. II. Title.
  GT4985.S36 2010
  394.2663—dc22

                                                        2009029676

Printed in the United States of America

10 9 8 7 6 5 4 3 2 1

Contents

Introduction

"Holiday family rituals may be annoying, but they are good for us."

—SYRACUSE UNIVERSITY STUDY

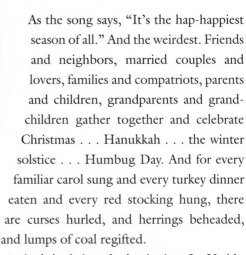

As the song says, "It's the hap-happiest season of all." And the weirdest. Friends and neighbors, married couples and lovers, families and compatriots, parents and children, grandparents and grand-children gather together and celebrate Christmas . . . Hanukkah . . . the winter solstice . . . Humbug Day. And for every familiar carol sung and every turkey dinner eaten and every red stocking hung, there are curses hurled, and herrings beheaded, and lumps of coal regifted.

And that's just the beginning. In *Upside-Down Christmas Tree: And Other Bizarre Yuletide Tales* you'll learn what truly strange goings-on go on behind closed doors in homes, towns, and nations around the world during the twelve days of Christmas. You'll meet people just like you who've created funny, freaky, and even frightening rituals to mark the happiest season of all. Like Carolyn in San Francisco, who, post-divorce, gave up the ghost of Christmas dinners past and fed her children barbecued chicken or pizza on Christmas; or Rain, an urban shaman in the Pacific Northwest, who spends her Christmas casting spells for her family members; or the Kellys from Houston, who spend their Christmas on the golf course, gifting each other with new balls; or the hundreds of *Seinfeld* fanatics who joyfully and irreverently celebrate the fabricated holiday Festivus by gyrating around a pole, airing their grievances, and wrestling each other to the ground, à la George Costanza's family; or Carol in Atlanta, who hosts an annual Barking Brunch, to which guests must bring their pooches and fuss over them as if they were children.

And you thought your family was weird.

Chapter One

ALL IN THE FAMILY

Antics Associated with the Holidays—Both Fun and Dysfunctional

Tolstoy's *Anna Karenina* begins, "All happy families are alike; each unhappy family is unhappy in its own way." And every year at Christmastime, American families prove Tolstoy right, again and again. Good behavior, bad behavior, outrageous behavior—the holiday season brings out the classy and the crass in all of us. From the sentimental to the, well, sick, what goes on behind closed doors on Christmas Day may surprise you. Then again, depending on your own family, it may not.

"MERRY CHRISTMAS, YOU'RE ARRESTED!"

Actions speak louder than words, especially at Christmas. So Laura from Northern California, a single mom whose ex owed her tens of thousands of dollars in back child support, decided to act decisively. The deadbeat dad had skipped town some eighteen months earlier, but Laura knew he'd sneak back to see his mother at Christmas. So she made sure that the local police knew where he'd be hanging out on Christmas Day, drinking beer and watching football with his moronic brothers while his elderly mother sweated over a hot stove making dinner for her middle-aged "boys." When the cops showed up with a warrant for his arrest, he tried to run out the back door, but he was apprehended nonetheless. Too bad for him—and too sweet for Laura. Now out of jail, her ex hasn't missed a child-support payment since, which means that this coming Christmas will be far more fun for Laura and the kids.

If you need to serve papers on someone, remember what Laura always says: There's no place like home for the holidays.

A WII BIT OF YULETIDE TROUBLE

Every holiday season Americans spend nearly $50 billion on electronics—and that's only at Christmas! That's a lot of cell phones, PDAs, big-screen TVs, and video games. (Some would say too many, but maybe they're just spoilsports, since electronic items are among the most desired of gifts.) But sometimes these highly prized presents cause as much pain as they do pleasure. Last year, a New Hampshire couple got into a real-time fight over a Wii. Heath Blom, 26, received a new Wii as a Christmas gift from his grandparents, with whom he and his girlfriend live. But Heath apparently was displeased by the expensive video game console. Unlike the millions of Americans clamoring for the Nintendo device, Heath really wanted a $1,000 remote-controlled airplane. He threw a tantrum (yes, we did say he was twenty-six years old), upsetting his grandparents. His girlfriend, Randi Young, 24, called him on his behavior, and in return he allegedly assaulted her. A brawl ensued, bruises were raised, and the cops were called. Upon inspection of the black and blue marks on both parties, the police arrested Randi and Heath on charges of domestic-related simple assault.

WARNING: NEVER OPEN YOUR PRESENTS EARLY

If you open your presents before Christmas, does that make you a criminal? According to one family in Rock Hill, South Carolina, it does. When Great-Grandma discovered that a present under the Christmas tree had been unwrapped and that the Nintendo Game Boy inside was missing, she told her great-grandson's mother and together they confronted the twelve-year-old. The boy denied taking the Game Boy, but after his mother threatened to call the police, he caved. The single mother, who'd been trying to deal with the boy's behavioral problems at home and school for some time, called the cops anyway. They charged the boy with petty larceny.

MAKE A LIST AND CHECK IT TWICE

Something weird was going on at a suburban duplex home outside Wilkes-Barre, Pennsylvania, in 2008. There were strange sounds coming from the attic, strange footprints in the closet in the master bedroom, and strange disappearances of household items. Was the place haunted by a Christmas ghost? Or was the mother of three who lived there simply imagining things? When cash, a computer, and an iPod went missing on Christmas Day, the homeowner called police. The next day, when she found footprints in the closet, she called again. The police brought along a search dog, who found an interloper living in the attic of the duplex.

Twenty-one-year-old Stanley Carter had been crashing with friends in the other side of the duplex; they'd asked him to

The Twelve Crimes of Christmas

Opening your presents early

Not getting your mom a present

Giving anyone *a fruitcake*

Serving eggnog sans *alcohol*

Working on Christmas Day—unless you're in public service

Really *stuffing your kids' stockings with coal*

Dieting on Christmas Day

Spending the entire day *watching football*

Returning everything *you get on December 26*

Spending the holidays alone more than two years in a row

Letting your loved ones spend the holidays alone more than two years in a row

Being so busy doing everything that you don't enjoy Christmas!

find a new place to live, and he disappeared. They filed a Missing Persons report shortly before the holiday.

Apparently Carter hadn't gone far. The duplexes shared an attic space—and he'd simply used a trap door to go from one side of the upper room to the other. He'd used the trap door in the mom's bedroom closet to enter her home, helping himself to food, clothing, and other household items. When he surrendered to police, he was wearing clothing the homeowner identified as belonging to her and her daughter. Carter was charged with criminal trespass, theft, burglary, and receiving stolen property. Police reported that they found a detailing of everything Carter had taken, entitled "Stanley's Christmas List."

THE FIGHTING TUPPERS

Christmas can be a stressful time—even for the happiest of families. That stress leads to overeating, overdrinking, and over-bickering. The Tupper family—known for their feuds—are an articulate, antagonistic bunch who view infighting as sport. For most of the year, they manage to keep a lid on it—mostly because they live fairly far from one another. But every Christmas they gather at the matriarch's home in Minnesota—and the battling begins. It's particularly bad during election years, as the family members' political views vary widely. There are dedicated Libertarians, left-of-left liberals, hard-core Republicans, Green Party members, and members of ACT UP, MADD, the AFL-CIO, NOW, the NRA, and DAR. They're a diverse group of dissidents and reactionaries, all of whom hold strong opinions and have no problem expressing them, loudly. Once the eggnog and bourbon is passed around and everyone's ego is well oiled, it's Loudmouths Gone Wild. The debating typically lasts throughout the cocktail hour, according to Mama Tupper, who calls a cease-fire when she rings the dinner bell. Once dessert is served, however, the fighting takes on a new intensity. Eventually the bickering devolves into name-calling, and people storm out—not to speak to one another again until Easter. It's a tradition the Fighting Tuppers are happy to continue forever.

MERRY *WHAT?*

Growing up in a Southern family from Georgia, Marilee and her sister and brothers were taught never to swear, particularly at the dinner table. Their mother held very high standards for all, but most particularly for the girls. A breach of propriety was equated to a criminal offense that their sainted mother would hold against them for months—or years. Thus, it was all the more surprising when Marilee went home one year, as a grown-up with two teenagers, and her sister not only breached the rules, she toasted them.

It began when Christmas tensions hit their peak and everyone's nerves were a tad raw. Marilee and her sister, Lynell, had been up well past 2:00 a.m. wrapping presents, trading stories, and drinking cheap wine, and eggnog for a nightcap. They had both woken up with hangovers and short fuses. For no reason that Marilee can remember, they started arguing with each other, the way sisters do, fussing about how to cook the bacon and eggs, how much nutmeg to add to the eggnog, and when they should put the turkey in the oven. Soon, they were inching closer to one of those little spats that so often accompany holiday mayhem. It just so happened that Marilee's two children and Lynell's two children were also in the kitchen—waiting for their bacon and eggs.

Inadvertently, Lynell called Marilee's son her son's name, and they all laughed—except Lynell. "Why are you laughing at me?" she asked.

"Because you called Jonathan Christopher," Marilee explained.

"I did not!"

"Well, yeah, you did, but it's no big deal," Marilee said.

A similar exchange continued for the next five minutes, until Lynell's two children chimed in: "Yeah, you called Jonathan Christopher." For some reason this pushed Lynell past her boiling point, and she flung the package of bacon on the counter and stormed out of the kitchen, shouting—very, very loudly—"Merry F***ing Christmas!"

Later, Lynell was mortified, of course, and made everyone concerned pinky-swear that they wouldn't tell her mother of her transgression. And they didn't—but for years afterwards, mostly because they spent Christmases alone, Marilee's teenagers would greet Marilee every Christmas morning with, "Merry F***ing Christmas."

In 2008, Marilee spent Christmas with Lynell and her family. When she called her homesick daughter, Grace, Marilee put Lynell on the line to issue what had become Marilee, Grace, and Jonathan's classic Lynell line. Lynell couldn't bring herself to repeat her signature line, but said, "Merry Freaking Christmas"—which made Grace laugh uproariously.

The beauty of family Christmases is that you can always beat a dead horse, embarrass your sister, and share a good laugh about the whole fiasco.

THE FAMILY THAT PRAYS TOGETHER

Lest we forget, Christmas is a religious holiday. That's one thing that the Merriweathers from Nebraska never forget. This devout family believes in the power of prayer—and they exercise that belief every day. This large extended family has formed a prayer circle devoted to the most worthy of causes. At Christmastime they redouble their efforts, praying for peace on earth and goodwill toward all, as well as for individuals who need help and have asked for their prayers. The Merriweather Prayer Circle reminds them of what is really important during this special time of year—and how lucky they are in so many ways. You, too, can form a prayer circle with your family and/or friends. Check out the Internet for instructions on how to get started.

THE SLEEPOVER CHRISTMAS

The women on *Sex and the City* got one thing right: When you've got girlfriends, you never have to spend the holidays alone; you just invite them for a sleepover. And if you're too depressed to invite anyone over, let them invite themselves— that's what friends are for. Maggie's boyfriend dumped her at Thanksgiving, and she was still a little shell-shocked when Christmas Eve rolled around. Too bereft to even get out of bed, the New Yorker planned on spending the holiday crying and napping, crying and napping, crying and napping. That's where her BFFs found her when they stormed the apartment. They came in and took over, making dinner, pouring wine, slipping Cher into the CD player. They brought lots of magazines and romance novels and nail polish, along with a basket full of presents. They put on their own pajamas, pulled Maggie out of bed, and force-fed her pasta and chocolate and cabernet and Lifetime movies. They made Maggie laugh through her tears when she opened their presents, which included a voodoo doll in the shape of her ex, complete with pins, and a Thunder from Down Under calendar for the new year. They stayed all night, and when Maggie woke up on Christmas Day, she felt happier than she had in a long time—if a little hungover.

AULD ACQUAINTANCE NEVER FORGOT

The ditty sung the world over on New Year's Eve is a masterpiece of sentimentality written by the famous Scottish poet Robert Burns in 1788 and set to an old folk song. We sing it every year as we remember the old and usher in the new. But sometimes our auld acquaintances are destined to reappear in our lives—on New Year's Eve. Harold and Margaret were high school sweethearts who drifted apart during college. They both went on to marry other people, live and work in different states, and raise families, losing track of one another somewhere along the way. Years later a mutual friend, knowing Harold was now a widower and Margaret was divorced, decided to secretly set them up on a blind date for a New Year's Eve party at her house.

Just like in the movies, they saw each other across their friend's crowded living room—and recognized each other immediately. By dessert it was obvious that the old chemistry was still there. At midnight they kissed as "Auld Lang Syne" played, and the years disappeared. Harold went home with Margaret that night and never left. But every New Year's Eve they throw an "Auld Lang Syne" party of their own to celebrate old friends and new love. You might want to look up a sweetheart of your own someday.

SPARE THE GRAVY

The year our friend Carolyn from San Francisco divorced, she wanted to prepare the same Christmas dinner she had served every year throughout her marriage. She didn't want her children—eight-year-old Gabrielle and six-year-old Spencer—to feel disappointed. She bought a twelve-pound turkey, fresh green beans, sweet potatoes, cranberries, stuffing—the whole shebang—and spent hours the night before and hours on Christmas Day prepping and cooking their traditional Christmas fare. But when they finally sat down to dinner, the children didn't fill their plates, but just nibbled on the homemade bread and mashed potatoes. After urging both to try this, and try that, and please at least take some of my famous sweet-potato pie—and being politely and consistently spurned—Carolyn lost her patience and ran to the bathroom, where she banged her fists on the bathroom door and cried.

From that holiday on, each Christmas Carolyn and her children plan their meals ahead of time—according to what they want to eat. One year they ate only hors d'oeuvres; the next they grilled chicken on the barbecue; another year, they

made pizza. And every year—saved from the agony of disappointment after hours spent preparing food they didn't want to eat anyway—they all have a good time playing games or watching movies.

IT'S RAINING GELT

Money—known as gelt in Yiddish—is a traditional Hanukkah present. The tradition dates to the sixteenth century, when Jewish parents in Poland sent their kids to *schul* with coins for their teachers at Hanukkah. The kids, being kids, insisted on some for themselves, and a new ritual was born. Today, both real coins and chocolate gelt often find their way into the hands of Jewish children everywhere during this eight-day holiday, thanks to parents and grandparents. In the Hasidic tradition, rabbis often give coins away to visitors during this time of year—a welcome gift believed to bestow blessings on the recipient.

You can bestow your own monetary and chocolate blessings on your favorite people: Invite your friends and family of all ages for a Gelt Toss. But don't just shower them with coins and candy; make them work for it. Set up containers—think pots and pans, Tupperware, etc.—in a corner of a room, and have kids and grown-ups alike try to sink their gelt into the containers from, say, ten feet away. What hits the mark, they get to keep. That's what the Rosenbergs do with their grandchildren every year in Boca Raton—and they love it.

Note to wealthy readers: If you've got the resources and you're feeling really generous, upgrade to paper money in large bills—and hide it throughout your home or yard. Now that's some *gut* gelt!

LATKE-EATING CONTEST

Food is an important part of every holiday—and that's as true of Hanukkah as anything else. Tasty traditional latkes—potato pancakes, fried in oil to commemorate the oil that miraculously burned for eight days—are a favorite with millions of Jewish families. But at the Kaufman house in Chicago, eating latkes is a sport. Every year the extended Kaufman family gathers at Nana Lilly's house on the North Shore to participate in the Latke-Eating Contest. Nobody makes latkes like Nana Lilly—and the fact that her relations are willing to stuff themselves with these delicious starchy treats until they puke is proof of that. Armed with the recipe from her Polish ancestors that has been passed down for generations, Nana Lilly and her daughters fry up hundreds of latkes—and the conspicuous consumption begins. Usually Uncle Morris, a stout insurance agent from Winnetka, wins by wolfing down more than six dozen of the high-fat, high-cholesterol, high-carb, high-calorie potato pancakes.

If you like latkes, host your own Latke-Eating Contest. Just be sure to stock up on prizes. Nana Lilly presents winners with brightly colored knit scarves for the long, cold Chicago winters—and lots of Alka-Seltzer.

Nana Lilly's Latkes   Serves 6 to 8

2 pounds of potatoes, peeled and grated
2 onions, peeled and chopped
2 eggs, beaten
Salt to taste
Cooking oil as needed

Mix together the first three ingredients. Using a spoon, drop 2-tablespoon scoops of the potato mixture into a hot skillet covered in a thin layer of the cooking oil. Press the mixture into patties and reduce heat to medium. Cook patties for 5 minutes on each side, or until brown. Drain on paper towels and salt to taste. Serve immediately.

Nana Lilly's Cooking Tip
If you're planning an eating contest, make latkes ahead and store them on a rack in a baking pan in the oven. When the contestants are ready, reheat the latkes at 350 degrees for five minutes, then remove and serve.

HANUKKAH SCAVENGER HUNT

If the thought of setting up carnival games in your home doesn't appeal to you, do what Nana and Papa Berger do with their family every Hanukkah in suburban Atlanta: They send their kids and grandkids out on a scavenger hunt. Every item on the to-be-found list is somehow related to Hanukkah—coins, dreidls, potatoes, candles, oil, etc. The people in the Bergers' neighborhood are by now used to the knocks on the door, which come when Bergers of all ages, from eight to eighty, ask for everything from cheese (think Judith of the Bible) to menorahs. The scavengers work in teams, parents and kids together. The winning family gets a trip to Disney World with Nana and Papa. Now that's a prize worth scavenging for!

THE CHOCOHOLIC'S HANUKKAH

Some people aren't satisfied with the little chocolate *gelt* distributed at most celebrations of Hanukkah. Our friend Amy of Dallas, a self-described chocoholic, says that Hanukkah is her favorite holiday—and she celebrates in a big cocoa-obsessed way. Amy hosts a wonderful Hanukkah party every year for all of her chocolate-loving friends, Jewish and otherwise. She has it catered by a company that specializes in chocolate fondue fountains. Guests gorge themselves, dipping fresh strawberries, banana slices, pineapple, kosher pound cake, brownies, cookies, pretzels, even mini-bagels and latkes, into several flavors of gourmet chocolate—including kosher chocolate. You can indulge in your own Chocoholic's Hanukkah. The easiest way: Simply hit your nearest gourmet chocolate store and stock up on your favorite candy. Take it home, light a candle on the menorah—and pig out. You can also make your own kosher chocolate fondue, slice up some fruit and other items, and invite your pals over for a kosher dip.

Kosher Chocolate Fondue

½ cup cocoa powder or 1 package Sephra Kosher chocolate chips
¾ cup sugar
½ cup margarine
½ cup soy milk or almond milk

Combine all ingredients in a heavy pan over medium heat. Stir continuously for 5 minutes, pour into fondue pot, and serve with fresh fruit, kosher cake, cookies, pretzels, and more.

OFF WITH THEIR HEADS HANUKKAH

One of the goriest stories associated with Hanukkah is the story of Judith, the beautiful widow who helped save the people of her hometown, Bethulia, from dying of thirst when the Assyrian general Holofernes surrounded the city, cutting off the water supply. Judith "surrendered" to Holofernes, then plied the love-struck general with wine and cheese. When he passed out she cut off his head and took it back to Bethulia with her. This bold move in turn motivated her people to fight back—and they did, with a vengeance.

If beheadings are more your style than spinning tops, host an Off with Their Heads Hanukkah. Our friend Nate, a Los Angeles Jew with a penchant for horror movies, invites all his twisted friends over every year for a Hanukkah Horror Film Fest. They hang out, ply themselves with wine and cheese à la Judith, and watch a marathon of films featuring beheadings.

Top Ten Beheading Movies

The Man Who Would Be King

Sin City

Il vangelo secondo Matteo (The Gospel According to St. Matthew)

Shaun of the Dead

Evil Dead II

The Evil Dead

Sleepy Hollow

Elizabeth

A Very Long Engagement

The Omen

Source: www.cinemagora.com

CHRISTMAS BY ANY OTHER NAME

It only figures that people would come up with playfully irreverent hybrid names for their unique Christmas celebrations. We found three that are a hoot.

Chrismukkah

Seth Cohen's character on the popular TV show *The O.C.* had a protestant mother and a Jewish father and thus, according to the storyline, created the hybrid Chrismukkah as a way for his family to celebrate Christmas and Hanukkah. They described it as "eight days of presents, followed by one day of many presents." The fictional family would put up a Christmas tree and a menorah, and spend Christmas Day watching *It's a Wonderful Life* and *Fiddler on the Roof* while eating Chinese takeout. The term caught on and led to a blitz of Chrismukkah products, including Chrismukkah T-shirts featuring reindeer with menorahs for antlers, Chrismukkah holiday cards extolling "Oy, Humbug" or "Chrismukkah in Jewtalia" (featuring a Leaning Tower of Pisa), and even an "Oy Joy" thong!

Chrismahanukwanzakah

Celebrated on December 13, *Chrismahanukwanzakah* was the brainchild of Virgin Mobile USA as a ploy for their 2004–2005 holiday advertising campaign. Blending Christmas, Hanukkah, and Kwanzaa, the ad satirized the effect of political correctness on the holiday season, using a song that proclaimed, "What matters most is camera phones for $20 less." The ad, featuring a variety of costumed people singing in the snow, scored Virgin Mobile USA an EFFIE Bronze Award for the Telecom Services category.

Festivus

Thanks to *Seinfeld*'s fictional George Costanza (played by Jason Alexander), Festivus has become a wacky holiday that many celebrate—just for the hell of it. George's fictional father, Frank (played by Jerry Stiller), created Festivus as a way for his family to let off holiday steam. He came up with the idea and coined the phrase "Festivus for the rest of us" after engaging in a tussle at a store over a doll. On December 23, the wacky Costanza family would erect a bare aluminum pole, which Frank praised for its "very high strength-to-weight ratio." The pole would remain unadorned, and no gifts were exchanged. Instead, they participated in what they called the Airing of Grievances, telling other family members how much they had disappointed them during the year, and practicing Feats of Strength, a ritual in which family members wrestled until the head of the household was pinned to the floor. *Seinfeld*'s final episode aired in 1998, and all these years later people still celebrate Festivus—in good-hearted fun. They raise glasses of Festivus Grape Ranch wine, or one of the four varieties of Festivus beer. They sing songs like "Gather 'Round the Pole" while dining on ham with a Junior Mint and Snapple glaze. Some even indulge in a little pole dancing.

Where It All Began

According to Allen Salkin, author of *Festivus: The Holiday for the Rest of Us* (Warner Books), real-life Festivus celebrations were held in ancient Rome and variations reignited in the mid-1960s in upstate New York, invented by the father of *Seinfeld* writer Daniel O'Keefe, a sociologist and *Reader's Digest* editor in Chappaqua, New York, who wanted to start a fun family tradition loosely based on ancient Roman festivals (Festivi).

Proving that Americans have embraced Festivus and celebrate it in good fun, here are some wacky spin-offs of Festivus:

- In 2000 and 2001, Ben & Jerry's featured a Festivus ice cream flavor. After a brief stint as Gingerbread Cookie, it has since been retired.

- During the 2000 football season, to keep his players focused on each game, Baltimore Ravens head coach Brian Billick banned his players from using the word "play-offs." His players substituted the term "festivus" for play-offs and "festivus maximus" for the Super Bowl. The Ravens won the Super Bowl that season.

- In 2004, during the last taping of his amazing run, *Jeopardy* mega-champion Ken Jennings and other contestants responded to clues about the holiday in a category entitled Festivus, part of a *Seinfeld*-themed round.

- In 2005, pole manufacturer the Wagner Companies of Milwaukee, Wisconsin, began producing Festivus poles.

- In 2005, after being dubbed "Governor Festivus," Wisconsin governor Jim Doyle displayed a Festivus pole in the family room of the Executive Residence in Madison. It's part of the collection of the Wisconsin Historical Museum.

- In 2007, the Santa Barbara Brewing Company created a winter ale they named Festivus: An Ale for the Rest of Us.

- Annually in early December, Connecticut College celebrates Festivus as a campus-wide formal event. They've added traditions, including the Spam and Keystone Party, in which participants eat as much spam and drink as much cheap beer as possible.

- In 2008, brothers Mike and Matt Tennenhouse erected a Festivus pole in the rotunda of the Illinois capitol in Springfield. They were "airing grievances" about governor Rod Blagojevich—on behalf of the people of Illinois, of course. The Illinois House was meeting just down the hall from the Festivus pole to discuss the start of impeachment proceedings.

QUASI-HOLIDAYS

According to *Chase's Calendar of Events*, the official keeper of all holidays—silly and otherwise—there are all manner of celebrations taking place throughout America all year. Those falling near Christmas include the following:

- December 21, Humbug Day: Faux-holiday legends Thomas and Ruth Roy created this day to allow those driven mad by the holidays a day to unload, or vocalize twelve "humbugs." The Roys also created Cat Herder's Day (Dec. 15), a celebration for anyone who believes their job, or their life, is as frustrating as trying to herd cats; Don't Step on a Bee Day (July 10); and Have-a-Bad-Day Day (Nov. 19), for those who are tired of hearing, "Have a nice day." The Roys have created more than sixty holidays, some as wild as Bathtub Party Day (Dec. 5).

- December 26, National Whiners' Day: Since 1986, some have designated this day as the day all the whiners who didn't like their Christmas gifts return them.

- December 28, Econo-Christmas Day: This is the day everyone who gave money to each other for Christmas goes shopping for bargains.

CHRISTMAS IS FOR THE BIRDS

Every year during the Christmas Bird Count, from December 14 to January 5, bird lovers from Miami to Montreal and beyond count birds for the National Audubon Society and Bird Studies Canada. Avid bird-watchers in some 2,400 North American communities gather on a given day during this aforementioned time period and count all the birds they can in that twenty-four-hour period. The counts help scientists monitor bird populations, and plan conservation efforts accordingly.

The Christmas Bird Count is the longest-running wildlife census in the New World—for more than 100 years, count circles of local bird-watchers have helped in this effort. Whether you live in the city or the country, you, too, can enroll yourself as a counter. In the United States, check out the National Audubon Society Web site; in Canada go to Bird Studies Canada/Etudes D'Oiseaux Canada.

Down for the Christmas Bird Count

Apart from helping out the birds, you'll also benefit you, yours, and your community. The Christmas Bird Count is a great way to

Involve the entire family
Go green this holiday
Meet fellow bird-lovin' locals
Hone your observation and listening skills
Learn more about your local flora and fauna
Get outdoors and enjoy nature

Source: www.eartheasy.com

THE GRINCH CHRISTMAS

The O'Malleys from New York don't like Christmas. They hate the crowds, the expense, the commercialism, the excess. They refuse to celebrate the holiday in the conventional American "more is more" way. So every year they have a Grinch Christmas. They don't exchange gifts or decorate a tree or roast a turkey. On Christmas Eve they watch *How the Grinch Stole Christmas*—and root for the Grinch. Then, on Christmas Day, they drive out of town to their cabin in the woods, where there's no evidence of the holidays whatsoever. They stay there

Our Top Five
"I Hate Christmas" Movies

How the Grinch Stole Christmas: Jim Carrey as Dr. Seuss's most terrible, quirky Scrooge.

Bad Santa: Billy Bob Thornton as the Santa from hell has never been better.

The Nightmare Before Christmas: A Tim Burton masterpiece of weird.

National Lampoon's Christmas Vacation: A Yuletide comedy of errors starring the Griswold family and its hapless patriarch, Chevy Chase.

Gremlins: What happens when you don't follow the instructions that come with your gifts.

through New Year's, not returning to civilization until the city is back to its normal pre-Christmas self. If you hate Christmas—and millions of us apparently do—have yourself a merry little Grinch Christmas!

THE CHRISTMAS PAGEANT

The Hubbles of rural Mississippi bemoan the lack of spirit in Christmas spirit these days. A religious couple whose marriage was grounded in faith, they wanted to ensure that their children understood the true meaning of Christmas. So they began an annual tradition dedicated to that effort. Not content to put a crèche under the tree, they constructed a life-size Christmas nativity on the expansive front lawn of their ten-acre country lot. They filled it with a manger, live sheep, and a donkey. They play the roles of the holy family, the shepherds, and the Magi, with a little help from their friends and neighbors. Usually they borrow a doll for the baby Jesus, but during official viewing hours on Christmas Eve a young mother with a baby always shows up to sit in as Mary and Jesus. It's Christmas as it was 2,000 years ago—and everyone loves it!

NEW YEAR, NEW MAN

After her second divorce, Emma from Oklahoma swore off men for a while. But eventually she knew that she had to get back on the horse, so to speak. She'd spent an average of ten years in a bad marriage that should have ended far sooner—*twice*. So she made herself a promise when she started dating again: Every New Year's Day she would take stock of her current relationship, and decide if she was really getting what she needed, if she really loved him, if she really knew who he was. And every New Year's Day she does just that.

Emma invites her girlfriends over, and they have a New Year, New Man brunch. They spend the afternoon drinking champagne punch, sampling hors d'oeuvres and desserts, and—most importantly—judging each other's men. There are scorecards for every relationship, which are filled out by the woman who's in the relationship as well as all the girlfriends. These scorecards address all aspects of the relationship—from courtesy and kindness to sex to fiscal responsibility. If he fails in only a few aspects, the girls brainstorm solutions. Any man who ranks unsatisfactorily across the board gets the boot. It's a system that works; having all the girlfriends in on the grading keeps everyone honest. Emma has said goodbye to a couple of guys, but her latest flame passed the test with flying colors. Happy New Year, indeed!

THE CAROLING WILBURYS

Okay, so their name really isn't Wilbury. But these singing kin from upstate New York know that at Christmas, it's the family that carols together that stays together. With Donna the music teacher as their muse, the Caroling Wilburys practice their Yuletide harmonies all autumn long in preparation for their "tour." They've mastered all the classic songs—"Silent Night," "Joy to the World," "Jingle Bells"—as well as modern classics like "Santa Baby," "White Christmas," and "All I Want for Christmas Is You." Their repertoire has grown over the years, much to the contentment of the many admirers who look forward to Christmas Eve, when the Caroling Wilburys take their show on the road. They walk an established route, going from house to house throughout the quaint seventeenth-century town in which they live. At every house along the way, the audience offers the performers treats and hot chocolate, and even brandy when it's very cold, as it is more often than not in New England in December. Their last stop: a local assisted living facility, where the patients provide the most welcome reception of all. It's a family tradition that keeps on giving, year after year, song after song.

Top Ten Most-Requested Christmas Songs to Be Played on the Radio

"Rudolph, the Red-Nosed Reindeer"

"Here Comes Santa Claus"

"I Saw Mommy Kissing Santa Claus"

"Winter Wonderland"

"Frosty the Snowman"

"I'll Be Home for Christmas"

"Silver Bells"

"Have Yourself a Merry Little Christmas"

"Santa Claus Is Coming to Town"

"The Twelve Days of Christmas"

CHRISTMAS CAMP

For those who love nature and hate the crass commercialism of Christmas—often the same people, according to our admittedly unscientific survey—setting up Christmas Camp is often the best option. Kate and Billy are two such nature lovers. To avoid the "Californication" of Christmas they get out of Los Angeles and head for greener pastures, going camping as far away from so-called civilization as they can. One of their favorite places to set up Christmas Camp is in rural New Mexico. Over the years they've invited like-minded souls to come with them to Christmas Camp—and now there's a core group of a dozen people who come every year. They sleep in tents, cook and eat outside, hike, sing carols around the fire under the stars. If you love camping, you might try hosting a Christmas Camp of your own. Just watch out for the rattlesnakes, mountain lions, and bears (oh, my).

CHRISTMAS FILM FESTIVAL

Christmas week consistently ranks as the highest-grossing week of the year for the film industry. One reason: Lots of great movies open this week, just in time to be considered for the Oscars. Another reason: Once everyone eats the turkey and opens all the presents, what else is there to do? And perhaps the most interesting answer: There are people for whom the movies are a religion— and for them Christmas is a holy day of a very different kind. Andrea, from Los Angeles, is a film fan who straddles both worlds: She loves Christmas and she loves movies. So instead of going to the movie theater, she throws her own Christmas Film Festival every year. She invites her fellow film nuts over and they eat popcorn and sip champagne while they watch the best of the holiday movies. Over the years, Andrea and her guests have watched everything from *The Christmas Carol* and *Scrooged* to *Eyes Wide Shut* and *Die Hard*. If you love movies, you may want to hold your own Christmas Film Festival. So much cooler than an Oscar party.

Our Top Ten Christmas Movies

It's a Wonderful Life

White Christmas

Love, Actually

A Christmas Story

Home Alone

Elf

Rudolph, the Red-Nosed Reindeer

Miracle on 34th Street

A Charlie Brown Christmas

The Santa Clause

BACK IN THE SADDLE CHRISTMAS

If you want to get away from people, Wyoming is a good place to start. The good news: In Wyoming, there are more deer than people, more antelope than people, more cows and sheep than people. The bad news: See above. (In case you don't know where Wyoming is, it's one of those big empty states in the middle. The one where Harrison Ford lives, in the Jackson Hole Valley.) Some say there are more cowboys than people, too, but those are the folks who are, to use a Wyoming expression, "all hat and no cow." If you like cowboys, then do what Janelle, from New York City, does every year. She packs up her Louis Vuitton bags and heads for a ranch in Wyoming, where she trades in her Donna Karan suits and heels for Wrangler jeans and boots and her BMW for a horse. She trades Christmas in a crowded city full of bankers for Christmas in the middle of nowhere—a very cold and windy nowhere—full of cowboys under a big sky full of stars. For Janelle, it's a Yippee Kai Yay Christmas!

Chapter Two

HOME FOR THE HOLIDAYS—*NOT!*

What People Will Do to Avoid Going Home for the Holidays

There may be no place like home for the holidays, but for a surprising number of people home is no place for the holidays. In fact, they go to great lengths to avoid home—and the people who represent home, for better or worse. (Mostly worse.) Their creativity knows no bounds—or boundaries. So if you keep finding yourself at yet another painfully boring/dysfunctional/psychotic family Christmas, it may be time to borrow one of these strategies.

THE WORKAHOLIC'S CHRISTMAS

The easiest way to avoid going home for Christmas: Just work right through it. "I have to work" is the most believable excuse in the world—even your mother will buy it. Especially if you are lucky enough to work in one of those positions that are on call 24/7, 365 days a year. Millions of cops, doctors, nurses, EMTs, firefighters, and convenience-store workers, among others, actually volunteer to work on major holidays—and not simply for the overtime pay. They do it to avoid going home on the homiest of days. An ER doctor we'll call David from Boston has missed the obligatory Christmas dinner at his folks' house now for six years running—with his parents' blessing. "Our son the doctor" is heralded for his humanity, even as his less-fortunate lawyer brother eats humble pie for five courses. For David, Christmas at home is more than he can bear, and he works through it by working through it. He couldn't do what his brother does; that would be more work than work could ever be. Don't feel too bad for his brother, though—David makes it up to him with box seats on Opening Day at Fenway every year.

Top Ten Reasons You Have to Work on Christmas That Even Your Mother Will Believe

You have a new client who's really high maintenance.

They're laying off half of your company's staff January 1 and you don't want to be one of them.

You're filling in for your boss who's getting married.

You're filling in for your colleague who's in the hospital.

You're working 24/7 to get that new promotion.

If you win this case, you'll make partner.

If you sign this deal, you'll get a huge commission.

You have a presentation to make on December 26.

You just got the job after being unemployed for six months—and you need to keep it.

Because it really is brain surgery.

BON VOYAGE, SANTA!

The easiest way to avoid your loved ones at Christmas is simply to leave town. This can be tough if you're on a tight budget, but one couple we know has Christmas on the Cheap down pat. Every year, they take the week of Christmas off, and take off for parts unknown. And when we say parts unknown, we mean it: They pack two bags each—one for a warm place, and one for a cold place. Then they go online and check out all the last-minute deals on the travel Web sites.

These packages are notoriously cheap, and surprisingly attractive. Ben and the Redhead from Philadelphia have been to the Caribbean, Europe, Mexico, Canada, and all over the United States—all for next to nothing. All it takes is an adventurous spirit and a call home on your way out of town to say, "Hasta la vista, Ma!"

CHRISTMAS MARATHON

If you want to run away from Christmas, you can. Just run! That's what runners Cary and Michael from Seattle do. It's a great excuse to avoid the holiday madness; they're so busy training and planning their marathon getaway that they miss the chaos altogether. They've run the Christmas Marathon in Olympia, Washington, the White Rock Half Marathon in Dallas, even the Standard Chartered Marathon in Singapore. All these races take place in December, and all are the perfect antidote to the hectic holiday season. So if you think running 26.2 miles just to avoid the Christmas rush is overkill, think again. You could just run your way to a brand-new Christmas high!

CALLING IN SICK FOR CHRISTMAS

Okay, so you wimped out and agreed to go to your family's annual Christmas gathering. You didn't want to go—you never want to go—but you caved, as usual. But now that Christmas is nearly here you cannot bring yourself to sacrifice another major holiday on the altar of family dysfunction. So wimp out again, and do what a woman we'll call Gwendolyn from Seattle does every year: Call in sick for Christmas. Gwendolyn may be as healthy as a horse, but her family would never know it. As far as they know, she suffers from chronic fatigue syndrome, asthma, fibromyalgia, and a seemingly continual series of colds, bronchial infections, and flus. You, too, could adopt a hypochondriac approach to Christmas—and turn December 25 into a sick day every year. Just remember to get plenty of rest and drink lots of fluids.

SCROOGED

If "bah, humbug!" sums up your attitude towards the holidays, then maybe what you need is not the attitude adjustment all your Christmas-crazy friends recommend, but rather to embrace the miserly old man in you. That's what a friend of ours from Los Angeles who shall remain nameless has done. Fed up with all the holiday hoopla, he's sworn off Christmas altogether. No presents, no family functions, no tree. He's informed all his friends and family that he doesn't do Christmas anymore—and he's happy with his choice. He saves himself a lot of grief—and a lot of money. So sue him.

The Money You Save
When You Skip Christmas

Turkey and all the trimmings　　$100

Christmas tree and wreath　　$75

50 Christmas cards　　$50

50 Stamps　　$22

New outfit for Christmas party　　$75

Entertaining　　$75

Christmas decorations　　$50

Gift for spouse　　$100 (if you're cheap)

Gift for kids　　$50 each (if you're really cheap)

Gift for Mom　　$50

Gift for Dad　　$50

Gifts for other family members　　$100

Gifts for non-family members　　$50

Wrapping　　$30

Total Saved　　$877 and up, depending on how many kids you want to disappoint.

CHRISTMAS IN PARIS

Sure, they always say that April is the time to go to Paris—but Christmas is pretty *formidable* in the fabled City of Light as well. The shopping is wonderful (and far less stressful compared to the U.S.!), the food is, well, French, and the Parisian Christmas spirit is one of a kind. Francophiles Carol and Rob spend every Christmas in Paris—giving them the annual Gallic fix they need and a much-needed change of pace from their hometown of Pittsburgh. Another plus: They're an ocean away from their high-pressure jobs as corporate attorneys, not to mention their parents, who never miss an opportunity to pester them about the grandchildren Carol and Rob are never going to give them. If you love Paris—and who doesn't?—you might want to consider spending the holidays there yourself. *Joyeux Noel!*

NO SPEAK CHRISTMAS HERE

If you live in the United States, there's really no getting away from Christmas. From Thanksgiving to New Year's, you're bombarded with holiday cheer—at the mall, on the street, even at work. Between crass commercialism on one hand and religious fervor on the other, Christmas is everywhere. So if you hate everything about this time of year, your only option for a true escape is to head to a place where they don't speak Christmas. For our intrepid high-minded friends Terry and Marlena from Seattle, that means places like Burma, Bhutan, Laos, and China. Or even Uzbekistan, Yemen, or Maldives. Just remember, if you go to a country where they don't celebrate Christmas, it may be a place they don't think much of Americans, either. Before you book your trip, visit *www.travel.state.gov* to check the U.S. government's list of current travel warnings. Note: At the time of this writing, there are twenty-eight countries on the list, including Yemen and Uzbekistan.

SPREAD YOUR LOVE AROUND

If you're married, you have a built-in excuse to bow out of at least every other Christmas gathering. By agreeing to alternate your trips home, you and your better half can each halve your familial pain. Millions of couples employ this very useful strategy, in the name of fairness to all (most especially themselves). If you're really lucky, you have more than two sets of parents, thanks to divorce and remarriage. If all four of your parents have remarried, then you can reduce your exposure to each parent significantly. One San Francisco couple we know, who understandably wishes to remain anonymous, has such a complicated family tree that between birth mothers and birth fathers, adoptive parents, stepparents, and step-grandparents on both sides of their families, they only have to visit each family domicile once a decade. So take up the mantle of equal time for equal relations, and spread yourselves around. You'll be glad that you did.

THE GOOD SAMARITAN CHRISTMAS

The spirit of Christmas is best exemplified by those who serve others during this most blessed time. These are the Good Samaritans who volunteer at soup kitchens, deliver hot Christmas dinners to shut-ins, play Santa to entertain sick children in hospitals, build homes for Habitat for Humanity, and more. A Midwestern gentleman known as Grambo is such a Good Samaritan; he selflessly donates his time and energy to a number of worthy causes all year, culminating in an orgy of good deeds at Christmas. This cornucopia of good works earns Grambo goodwill, good self-esteem, and good reason to miss whatever holiday-related functions he chooses to miss. Sign up as a Good Samaritan, and you can pull a Grambo, too.

HAVE YOURSELF AN ENLIGHTENED LITTLE CHRISTMAS

In the midst of all the "X Number of Shopping Days Left Before Christmas" madness, we sometimes forget that Christmas is, at its heart, a religious holiday. Remember this, and you may find the most blessed means of missing Christmas at home that ever was, is now, or will be. Sign yourself up for a spiritual retreat, and take yourself off to save your soul for Christmas. Shakti, a spiritual seeker from Northern California, spends every holiday season at a different retreat. For her it's grace of the karmic kind—she can avoid her family and achieve enlightenment at the same time. She's been to every holy hot spot in the West. From the hot tubs of Esalen and Marin to the harmonic convergences of Mount Shasta and Sedona, Shakti has enjoyed a little Yuletide satori every year since the dawning of the new millennium . . . and counting.

Spiritual Retreats to Satori By

The Insight Meditation Center of Pioneer Valley, Massachusetts

Omega Institute, New York

Esalen Institute, California

Kripalu Center, Massachusetts

Mount Madonna Center, California

Breitenbush Hot Springs, Oregon

Ala Kukui, Hawaii

Angel Valley, Arizona

Shambhala Mountain Center, Colorado

SPLIT AND RUN

Every family wants to be together at Christmas—and the pressure is often on couples to accommodate each of their family's desires. For those husbands and wives who have never been truly accepted by their in-laws, such family functions can be uncomfortable. But Nick and Nora of New York City have figured out a way to keep their families happy without sacrificing their dignity or their self-respect as individuals or as a couple. They call it Split and Run. Every Christmas Eve, Nick and Nora split up. He goes to his family in Queens, and she goes to her family in New Jersey. They satisfy their obligations to their families, and they meet back in Manhattan for their private Big Apple Christmas celebration. This way everybody's happy— and Nick and Nora save the very best for last.

THE MERRY MONKS
OF DECEMBER

If your religious tastes run along more conventional Christian lines, then you can skip the obligatory family Christmas dinner and prove to your mother that you really love Jesus at the same time by spending Christmas at a monastery. There are monasteries all over the world that accept overnight guests for days, weeks, even months at a time. One former Irish-American seminarian of our acquaintance became a divorce lawyer instead of a priest, but he still books himself into a Benedictine monastery every Christmas nonetheless. This allows him to recharge his spiritual batteries in anticipation of the busiest time of the year for the divorce business (January), excuse himself from his family Christmas dinner, and refresh his poor faithful mother's hope that he may eventually see the error of his ways and return to the seminary.

Monasteries to Pray By

Our Lady of the Mountain Retreat House, Utah

St. Meinrad Archabbey, Indiana

Monastery of Christ in the Desert, New Mexico

Blue Cloud Abbey Retreat Center, South Dakota

Benet Pines Retreat Center, Colorado

Red Plains Spirituality Center, Oklahoma

Holy Name Monastery, Florida

Glastonbury Abbey, Massachusetts

House of Bread Monastery, British Columbia

St. Cecilia's Abbey, Isle of Wight

Abbaye Saint-Marie de Maumont, France

Foresteria del Monastero S. Scolastica, Italy

WINTER SOLSTICE WITH THE WITCHES

Opting out of Christmas is easy when you're a witch. Witches celebrate the winter solstice (when the sun shines down on the Tropic of Capricorn on December 21 or 22 in the Northern Hemisphere) rather than Christmas, so you'll be off in the woods watching the sun rise and set while the rest of your family is at home opening presents they don't need or want and watching football. There are a number of different pagan traditions you can explore, including Wicca. A witch known as Rain, from the Northwest, started her own coven and spends every winter solstice in the bosom of her new Wiccan family. She casts spells for friends and family—new and old—as a gesture of goodwill for New Year's. Another plus: Her devout Christian mother stopped inviting her to Christmas dinner, convinced that she practices black magic. Which she doesn't—but what her mother doesn't know won't hurt her.

Happy New Year's Spell

Write out your New Year's resolution on a piece of paper. Then wait for the first new moon of the new year and do one of the following two things. If you want to break a bad habit—give up smoking, leave your loser lover, quit your dead-end job—then burn that paper with a red candle, and release the ashes into the night air. If you want to do something new and good—find true love, move to Hawaii, change careers—then take that piece of paper and put it in a special, secret place. Blessed be!

> ## Spiritual Retreats for Jews Around the World
>
> *The Elat Chayyim Center for Jewish Spirituality, Connecticut*
>
> *Bnei Baruch Learning Center Kabbalah Retreat, Missouri*
>
> *Chochmat HaLev (Wisdom of the Heart), California*
>
> *Kibbutz Lotan, Israel*
>
> *Neve Sha'anan Yoga Center, Israel*

HOLY HANUKKAH HIATUS

Hanukkah is the Hebrew word for dedication—referring to the rededication of the temple in Jerusalem in 165 BC which the holiday celebrates. Given that, the so-called Festival of Lights is the perfect time for Jews looking for a little spiritual renewal–and time away from Aunt Mildred's heavy-as-a-door-stop latkes—to go on a retreat. Our friend Josh from New York escapes the city and the annual Cousins Club Hanukkah get-together by heading off for a soulful retreat. He's studied the Torah with a *rosh yeshiva* in Connecticut, explored the mysteries of the Kabbalah in Spain, and worked on a kibbutz in Israel. Josh comes back refreshed, renewed, and revitalized physically, mentally, and spiritually. It's a mitzvah for himself. You can self-mitzvah, too—just pack your bags and your menorah and hit the road for a Gut Yontif!

HAVE A HAPPY JEWBU HANUKKAH

JewBus are Buddhists of Jewish descent . . . or Jews studying Buddhism . . . or both trying to integrate spiritual principles of both traditions. (Which reminds us of a joke our beloved friend Carl Bergman used to tell us, which goes something like this: Two Jews, three opinions.) Our favorite self-described JewBu, Brian from Maine, spends his Hanukkahs at the Kripalu Center in western Massachusetts, doing yoga, meditating, chanting, and studying holy texts with a rabbi. If you find yourself lighting menorahs and quoting the Dalai Lama at the same time, you might enjoy a JewBu Hanukkah yourself. Take a Right Action and book yourself into one of the many spiritual centers where you're likely to encounter like-minded Jews in search of enlightenment. You won't be alone; according to Rodger Kamanetz, poet and author of *The Jew in the Lotus,* a full 50 percent of Westerners visiting the Dharamsala-based Vipassana meditation retreats are Jewish. *Oy vey* and *aha!*

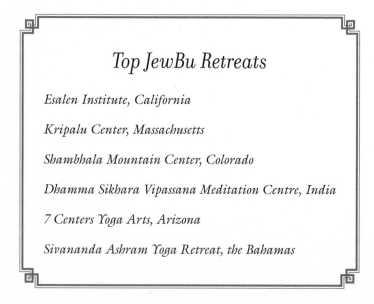

Top JewBu Retreats

Esalen Institute, California

Kripalu Center, Massachusetts

Shambhala Mountain Center, Colorado

Dhamma Sikhara Vipassana Meditation Centre, India

7 Centers Yoga Arts, Arizona

Sivananda Ashram Yoga Retreat, the Bahamas

CHRISTMAS HAWAIIAN STYLE

Way up in the Northeast, close to the Canadian border, Christmas is a snowbound affair. And it's just the beginning (middle?) of a very long winter. Spring is a *long* way off . . . so the New Englanders who don't really like cold weather (yes, there are a few) sometimes start their new year with a trip to Hawaii or the Caribbean. Those who can't "away" to a tropical island throw themselves a little Caribou Christmas Luau. They don Hawaiian shirts over their long johns, roast a pig, and dance to a little Don Ho. If you're thinking that you can't roast a pig in the snow, think again. Yankees can roast anything, anywhere, no matter what the weather. If they're feeling lazy, they call an outfit like Avermonter Enterprises in Killington, Vermont, whose slogan is, "We travel to you." They specialize in Vermont pig roasts, racks of lamb, and racks of ribs.

You don't have to live in God's country—north of the forty-fourth parallel—or be buried in snow to hold your own luau. No matter where you live, you can go hog wild for Christmas. Just don't forget the Hawaiian Shirt Contest, the Hula Dance-Off, or the poi.

Christmas Poi

1 pound taro root
Water

Boil the taro roots until soft. Peel and cut into bite-sized pieces. Mash while warm. Add water and stir until thickened. Serve cold or at room temperature with salt, sugar, or soy sauce.

MAMA'S CRUISIN' CHRISTMAS

Sometimes it's not home so much as it is dear old Mom that sends people packing as December 25 approaches. Especially when Mom is old and alone and looks to her children and grand-children to fill the void left behind in her oh-so-very empty nest/condo. One Maine family, whom we'll call the Wilsons, even-tually tired of the perennial tug-of-war that characterized every Yuletide. Mom tugged, and they pulled, and after years of "you take her; no, you take her" everyone finally realized that what their widowed Mom wanted was not so much to spend every minute of every day of every December with her family, but rather to not spend it alone. So the Wilson kids chipped in and booked Mom on a Christmas cruise for seniors to the Caribbean. Mama Wilson had a ball with her own kind—dancing, playing bridge, and making lots of friends (including a male companion named Jack)—and the rest of the Wilsons celebrated their first hassle-free, Mom-free Christmas since their beloved Dad passed. They loved their Mom, but they loved her even more when she got a life. Now she asks for a cruise every year for Christmas—and every year she gets one. She's been to the Bahamas, Ber-muda, and Key West, with her devoted Jack in tow. And when she comes back, she always invites the family over for Mama's Cruisin' Christmas slide show. And they all come.

GOLF IF YOU LOVE JESUS

Couples who golf together stay together—every day of the year. For couples who love golf as much as they loathe traditional holidays, spending Christmas on the green is the answer. The Kellys of Houston are one such couple. Childless by choice, they'd rather skip the rug rat–infested family holidays on both sides of their families by skipping out of town to the luxury golf resort of their choice. They give themselves the gift of

Faraway Golf Courses

Thimphu, Bhutan

St. George, Bermuda

Canmore, Alberta

Ballybunion, Ireland

Kingston Heath, Australia

Pevero, Sardinia

St. Andrews Links, Scotland

Valderrama, Spain

Penina, Portugal

Falsterbo Golfklubb, Sweden

Fuchun, China

Phoenix Country Club, Japan

Laguna Phuket Golf Club, Thailand

Leopard Creek, South Africa

Lagunita Country Club, Venezuela

the holidays alone together doing the thing they love most in the world (besides each other). Their families may groan, but in time they've grown to accept the couple's annual absence, chalking it up to golf madness. They even present the golf-crazy Kellys with a stocking full of golf balls every year—and never even suspect that golf is just an excuse to spend Christmas far, far away from home.

RUFFIN' IT

They say that dogs are a man's best friend. And for those of us who'd prefer to be among animals rather than people every crazy, chaotic, stressful holiday season, that's especially true. You can hide out from friends and family yet not be lonely if you have your dog to keep you company. Stock up on dog treats and toys for Rover, and human treats and toys for you. Spend the Yuletide taking long walks in the park or in the woods or on the beach, playing fetch, and pigging out on meat products. Indulge in a movie marathon featuring films you'll both enjoy—*Marley & Me, Call of the Wild, Turner & Hooch*—or just tune in to Animal Planet. When dog lover Ben S. moved to New York right before the holidays and found himself alone in that big city with no one but his Doberman, he ruffed it out with Duke—and it turned out to be one of his happiest Christmases ever. If you don't have a dog, volunteer to dog sit for loved ones going out of town for Christmas. Better yet, give yourself the gift of a precious pooch for Christmas by adopting a dog from your local animal rescue center—*then* you can ruff it 365 days a year.

GONE TO THE DOGS CHRISTMAS

If you love dogs and dog people, throw a New Year's Barking Brunch. Our friend Carol, Atlanta-based events planner extraordinaire, hosts several dog parties a year, but nothing beats her Barking Brunch. This annual event gets the new year off to a rollicking start for her, her Scottie named Jazz, and all her dog and human friends. She decorates doggie style—turning her house and yard into a heavenly canine haven. It's Southern hospitality gone to the dogs with a Fido-friendly menu of grilled burgers, hot dogs, and ribs. The humans imbibe their own special Hair of the Dog bourbon punch while the dogs chow down, race around, and compete in a variety of doggie games. There are agility contests, Frisbee-catching competitions, eating contests—and even a Best-Dressed Dog costume contest. The most hilarious events: the Human-Dog Talent Show and Karaoke Howl-Off.

Host your own Barking Brunch this New Year's—your dog will love you for it!

DIVIDE AND CONQUER CHRISTMAS

Couples who dread visiting each other's families—not to mention their own—can join forces to get through the holidays in the most efficient and least emotionally draining way possible. That's what Jill and Brian from Denver do. They visit his family first, dropping by for the obligatory Christmas brunch at his parents' house. They stick close to one another, which allows Jill to waylay Brian's critical father with her charm whenever the old man starts hurling insults at Brian. Brian repays the favor at Jill's parents' place later that afternoon, when they arrive for her family's annual Christmas dinner. The elaborate meal always starts with martinis, which Jill's mother always enjoys to excess. By the time she's had three, she's harping on Jill's failure to produce a grandchild. That's when Brian steps in and steers his mother-in-law back to the kitchen, where he helps her prepare the platters and bring them to the table. He sits next to her at dinner, allowing Jill to steer clear of her mother and enjoy a pleasant meal sitting next to her easy-going father. By dessert, they beg off and go home, each grateful to the other for having helped to make the best of a bad situation. Safe at home they can have their own private Christmas, just the two of them. If you and your mate have similarly dysfunctional families, you can enlist each other's aid to get through the day as pleasantly as possible. All you need is a little back-up—from one another!

Playing Hooky from Family Christmas Movies

If you don't have the nerve to skip the family Christmas get-together, try watching one of the following films for a little inspiration. It'll remind you why you really should bail this year.

Home for the Holidays

Four Christmases

The Ice Storm

The Ref

The Family Stone

Chapter Three
ALL THE TRIMMINGS

If It's Standing Still, Decorate It!

Christmas is a time of celebration—and nothing says celebration like decoration! Christmas with all the trimmings is an elaborate affair—and an expensive one. Americans spend nearly $500 million a year on Christmas trees—the real ones—and millions more on fake trees. We spend nearly $10 billion a year on Christmas decorations. And another $4.3 billion on Christmas cards. Not to mention all the home-grown decorations people make themselves, the materials for which run us another $44.9 billion a year. That's a lot of green for a little red and green. But it wouldn't be Christmas without it, now would it?

People go to enormous expense and lengths to make their Christmas beautiful. But at Christmas, as at every other time of the year, beauty is in the eye of the beholder.

THE MEANING OF CHRISTMAS TREES

The first written record of a decorated Christmas tree dates to 1510 in Riga, Latvia. Men belonging to the local merchants' guild decorated a tree with artificial roses, danced around it in the marketplace, and then set fire to it. The rose was used as a decoration for many years and is still considered to be a symbol for the Virgin Mary. So in honor of Our Lady of Christmas, let your tree "bloom" with silk roses this year!

O TANNENBAUM, POSSUM STYLE

Some say "to-MAY-to," some say "to-MAH-to," and some say, "hang 'em upside down" instead of "hang 'em high." Back in the Middle Ages, European Christians hung their fir trees upside down at Christmastime to represent the Trinity. As time went on, though, the Trinity lost out to heaven itself; since Christmas trees are shaped with the tip pointing skyward, hanging it upside down seemed disrespectful or sacrilegious to many. So the tradition, uh, reversed itself.

Fast forward to the twenty-first century, in which topsy-turvy trees are once again gaining on their straight-up counterparts. This renewed popularity is attributed to those most dedicated of holiday revelers, retailers—who turned the tables on the trees for their in-store displays. Whether they did this out of genuine Christmas cheer, to dangle high-priced ornaments at the buying public's eye level, or simply to provide more floor space to show off more decorations, only Santa Claus knows for sure. But the upside-down Christmas trees have caught on, and are now being sold to the public as a novelty piece, and— surprise, surprise—not cheaply! Target sells a pre-lit one for a whopping $399, and upscale retailer Hammacher Schlemmer reports that they can't keep their version in stock. Even the discount retailer Sam's Club offers a Seven-Foot Upside-Down Pre-Lit Christmas tree for your viewing pleasure.

A smile may be a frown turned upside down, but in today's America, a Christmas tree is just a holiday bush, any way you hang it. At least in public.

Set That Tree on Fire, Monsieur!

The first accounts of using lighted candles as decorations on Christmas trees come from France in the eighteenth century.

Sell That Tree, Monsieur!

The first recorded sale of a Christmas tree occurred in Alsace, France (then part of Germany), in 1530. Trees were purchased in the marketplace, brought home, and set up undecorated. Laws limited the height to "eight shoe lengths," or slightly more than four feet.

IF YOU CAN EAT IT, STRING IT

In parts of Austria and Germany in the 1700s, evergreen tips were brought into the home and hung top down from the ceiling. They were often decorated with apples, gilded nuts, and red paper strips. Edible ornaments became so popular that Christmas trees became known as sugar trees.

Make your own sugar tree:

Hang candy canes
String popcorn and cranberries
Hang chocolate-covered pretzels with ribbon
Make gumdrop ornaments (with gumdrops and toothpicks)
Make licorice and Life Savers rings (thread licorice with Life Savers and tie at the top)

TRIM A YEE-HAW CHRISTMAS TREE

If you spend your holidays wassailing in the cow pasture, you may be the perfect customer for a truly unique Christmas tree. It's just a little bitty thing, constructed of barbed wire and designed to sit on a tabletop. The base is a rusted horseshoe (miniature, of course), from which barbed wire spirals upward. It's ten and a half inches wide at its widest point and twenty-six inches high and topped with a rusted star. It's minimalism, cowboy style, and sure to please you or the wrangler in your life.

Accoutrements to be found online include a Christmas star made out of rope, a barbed-wire garland, and cowgirl-gear ornaments. You can find rusted ornaments in the shape of a cow skull or cowboy boots, and if you're a gun enthusiast, you can light it up with a strand of twenty lights made from actual buckshot shells! Just be careful when you hang the ornaments or you may get snagged.

Evergreen Druids

The druids in ancient England and Gaul (France) and the Romans in Europe used evergreen branches to decorate their homes and public buildings to celebrate the winter solstice, and signal the return of vegetation at winter's end. In addition to evergreen boughs, they decorated with holly, laurel, ivy, mistletoe, rosemary, and laurel—and later Christmas trees.

Lights, Mr. Edison!

Electric tree lights were first used just three years after Thomas Edison had his first mass public demonstration of electric lights back in 1879. The early Christmas tree lights were handmade and quite expensive.

TRIP THE LIGHTS FANTASTIC

You've heard of going green—well, at the Enshima Aquarium in Kanagawa, Japan, they've gone sea-green! At the aquarium they used an unusual source to light a Christmas tree—and that's putting it mildly. After installing two aluminum panels in a freshwater tank to act as electrodes, the museum brought in an electric eel to light their tree. That's right—an electric eel. Every time the eel moved, he generated 800 watts of electricity that blinked the Christmas tree's lights. Kazuhiko Minawa, the genius behind the idea, said he fantasizes about gathering all the electric eels on the planet to power an unimaginably large Christmas tree. "I'd love to see the huge flash of light it would make on earth from somewhere in the universe."

A FISHY CHRISTMAS

If you think that a fishing Christmas theme is a little tacky, think again. After all, many of Jesus's disciples were fisherman, including St. Peter himself. And the fish has been a symbol of Christianity since the early days. So if your husband wants to wrap your Christmas in fish, you just may have to let him, like Norma from Arkansas did. Her husband, Daryl, redecorated the house for Christmas, replacing her snowflake theme with a "gone fishing for God" motif. Daryl, an avid fisherman, decked his halls with colorful fishing flies and fishermen's nets. He trimmed the tree with ornaments shaped like rainbow trout, fishing reels, and even the odd rod or two. He swapped out the angel and crowned the tree with a misshapen fisherman's hat. Dressed in his red Santa hip waders, Daryl oversees the Annual Lighting of the Fish Tree. Encircled in lots of strings of bass lights, the Fish Tree is a sight to be seen—from across the lake.

Sing for Your Salvation

The fish as a symbol for Christianity is alive and well and being sung as we speak. The Christian a cappella group Go Fish features an original song called "Christmas with a Capital C" on their first holiday album, A Go Fish Christmas.

CHRISTMAS THINGS THAT GO POOP IN THE NIGHT

Apparently there is a market for everything, and people with a juvenile sense of humor love poop—even at Christmas. You can find a host of Christmas-themed ornaments or playthings whose one big attraction is that they, well, poop. You buy the plastic wonder in your choice of guise—Santa Claus, polar bear, reindeer, sheep, penguin, or apparently whatever your funny bone desires. Then you, too, can surprise Aunt Sophia at Christmas dinner when you push Santa's little head down and "poop" emerges to the delight of all.

The poop, by the way, is edible. It's sweet poop, if you will—candy shaped like little pellets. And if that's not graphic enough, you can also find ornaments shaped like poop called *Yule Doos.*

Fake It Until You Decorate It

Sears, Roebuck and Co. offered the first artificial Christmas trees, with thirty-three limbs for 50 cents and fifty-five limbs for $1, in the late 1880s.

PRAISE THE LORD AND PASS THE AMMUNITION

For many patriotic Americans, NRA members, and Call of Duty video-game enthusiasts, a war-themed Christmas is the way to go. If you, too, prefer "an eye for an eye" to "turn the other cheek," take a cue from our friend Frank from Michigan. Frank is a WWII veteran who's been collecting military-style Christmas decorations since he survived Pearl Harbor. His den is a veritable museum of present and past conflicts. From the Corning Glass Works' machine-blown glass balls painted with stars and stripes that debuted shortly after World War II began to the ornaments shaped like bin Laden's head, you can trace the history of American warfare just by perusing the tree. You'll find Santa there too, riding high on tanks and helicopters— and if you're a good shot, try taking Santa out by lobbing one of the nearby grenade ornaments at him. Just don't let Frank catch you—or you could find yourself hanging from the tree yourself.

GREEN CHRISTMAS

Christmas may be the best part of the year, but it's also the trashiest time of year. Americans alone generate some two billion tons of additional garbage every week during the Christmas season, starting with Thanksgiving. And most of it sits in landfills, taking eons to decompose. But you can take your cue from millions of eco-aware citizens and cut down on your Christmas footprint by adopting some simple greening tips and tricks.

Top Ten Easy Ways to Go Green at Christmas

You may not be ready to go as green as the Barkleys of Washington State—whose greening efforts include adopting a vegan diet, forgoing all Christmas gifts, and installing a composting toilet—and that's okay. There are less extreme ways to benefit the earth—and still save money as well.

Use LED lights. They're 90 percent more efficient—and you won't have to replace them as often, either.

Buy a live, potted tree, which you can plant outside later.

Swap out traditional gift items for gift experiences, such as guitar lessons, theater tickets, museum memberships, etc.

(Continued)

Forgo paper wrapping for reusable containers, such as baskets, wooden boxes, and cloth bags.

Spend Christmas at your house. No travel means no gas emissions from planes, trains, and automobiles.

E-mail your season's greetings. It's cheaper, faster, and far more eco-friendly.

Light up a soy candle. These environmentally correct candles smell just as good and come in just as many forms—tapers, pillars, votives, floating types—as their conventional counterparts.

Make your own organic decorations. Take the kids on a nature walk and gather pine cones, seashells, or evergreen branches. Or help them make homemade decorations out of recycled paper, fabric scraps, and more. You'll only be limited by your imagination!

Always carry (and use) reusable shopping bags—and not just at Christmas, but every day of the year.

Donate whatever you can to charity. Clean out your garage, your attic, your closets—and give away whatever someone else might be able to use. You can give monetary donations as well. After all, it's the giving season!

Source: www.thegogreenblog.com

GO GREEN HANUKKAH

Bemoaning the ecological impact of the millions of Hanukkah candles burned every year during the holiday, a group of Israeli environmentalists have started a Green Hanukkah campaign designed to persuade Jews around the world to light at least one fewer candle every year. Lighting the menorah, a nine-branched candelabrum, is a vital part of the tradition. Every night of the eight nights of the holiday, another candle is lit—each candle releasing fifteen grams of carbon dioxide per night into the atmosphere. By not lighting the *shamash*, the ninth candle used to light the other eight candles, representing the eight days of Hanukkah, Jews can reduce the Hanukkah footprint.

"The campaign calls for Jews around the world to save the last candle and save the planet, so we won't need another miracle," says Liad Ortar of the Arkada environmental consulting firm.

A worthy ambition—but one that has its detractors. "This is so trivial, so anti-Jewish and so anti-religious that even the worst anti-Semites couldn't think of it," says Israeli politician Shas MK Nissim Ze'ev. "Just like the Hellenists, they are trying to extinguish the flames of the Jewish soul."

So go green if you dare—and save the planet, one candle at a time.

SUPER-SIZE YOUR CHRISTMAS

Some people just can't get enough fast food—even on Christmas. While the rest of us are feasting on homemade turkey and stuffing, Christmas goose and plum pudding, pecan pie and fruitcake, these Big Mac maniacs are drowning themselves in fast food—both literal and figurative. These drive-thru aficionados proclaim the glories of fast food in every possible way. They trim their trees with ornaments in the shape of cheeseburgers, french fries, tacos, slices of pepperoni pizza, fat bottles of Coke, bottles of Hershey's Syrup, cinnamon buns, peanut butter and jelly sandwiches, hero sandwiches, and outdoor barbecues.

If you can't guess what's on the menu for Christmas dinner, you must be in a fast-food coma. At one artery-clogger's house, you'll find burger lover Big Mac (aka MacArthur) and all his burger-loving pals washing down KFC Original Recipe fried chicken, Whoppers, curly fries, chili dogs, burritos, Meat Lover's pizzas, McNuggets, Hershey's Sundae Pies, and doughnuts with Bud Light. Lots of Bud Light.

WORK-AT-HOME CHRISTMAS

For those who always take their work home with them, a career-themed Christmas is a wise (if weirdly workaholic) choice. Here are some tips on how your favorite job-obsessed careerist can make the most of his or her chosen occupation every holiday season.

A Very Hairy Christmas

Give your salon tree a trim: Hang bright-colored rubber hair rollers, pretty hair clips, and ribbons on the branches. Top off the tree with a yellow wig, add a HAIR TODAY, BLONDE TOMORROW sign, and string miniature hair dryers, travel bottles of shampoo, and cute little combs and hair brushes around the tree. When it's time to take the tree down, all you need to do is invite your clients to take an ornament/present home with them!

Farmer John Grows a Tree

Approximately twenty-five to thirty million real Christmas trees (as opposed to artificial trees) are sold each year in the United States. Almost all of these come from Christmas tree plantations. There are close to half a billion real Christmas trees currently growing on Christmas tree farms in the United States alone, all planted by farmers.

The Teaching Tree

There are three million teachers in American public schools alone—and everyone knows they're underpaid and underappreciated. What better way to show your appreciation for the teacher in your life—even if it's you!—than to decorate your Christmas tree in honor of the teaching profession. Trim it with pencils and erasers, little red plastic apples, and tiny books and bookmarks. Add sheet music and musical notes for music teachers, rulers and plastic numbers for math teachers, postcards of famous writers and red pens for English teachers, and miniature footballs and baseball bats for gym teachers. Trim a tree for your teacher—and move to the head of the class.

Under-Construction Tree

If there's a tradesperson in your home, stop bugging him or her to remodel the kitchen. If a picture is worth a thousand words, then an Under-Construction Christmas Tree will be the ultimate reminder. No matter whether you're living with a carpenter, builder, contractor, plumber, painter, or electrician, all you need to do is make a trip to your local hardware store and/or toy store, and you're good to go. You'll find all the real—or toy—nails, paintbrushes, wiring, hammers, pipe, and blueprints you need to turn your tree into a Yuletide work in progress. It couldn't be easier—because you don't even have to finish it by Christmas!

To Your Good Health Christmas

If you don't count any health-care workers among your loved ones now, odds are you will soon: The U.S. Department of Labor predicts that 2.4 million new health-care workers will be hired in the next five years. You can do your part to say thank you to your favorite nurse, doc, or physician's assistant by trimming your tree with good health in mind. Raid your kids' doctor kits, Operation games, and nurse costumes for inspiration, add your own (empty) pill bottles, hot-water bottles, and bandages and give that tree the rubdown it deserves. To your health!

An Apple a Play

In the fourteenth and fifteenth centuries, evergreen boughs hung with apples were used in the miracle plays that were performed at churches on December 24. In those days, December 24 was Adam and Eve's Day. Miracle plays were the primary way Christians taught the Bible to a largely illiterate population.

Spruce Up Your Christmas

W. V. McGalliard created the first Christmas tree farm when he planted 25,000 Norway spruce on his farm in New Jersey in 1901.

THE FAMILY TREE

For many of us, Christmas is all about family. And for the nineteen million of us who're tracing our family trees and the 113 million who want to, a Family Tree might be the sentimental favorite of all themed Christmas trees in America. There are many ways you can honor your family—past and present—by decorating your tree. Our friend Maggie, from Boston, is Irish, and she's traced her family back to the Great Famine, when her ancestors left Cork for the United States. She trims her tree with framed photos of her family members—kids, grandkids, siblings, parents, aunts, uncles, and grandparents, all the way back to great-great-great-great-grandparents. She strings shamrock lights and adds Celtic crosses, postcards of Ireland, and lots of bright green balls. It's a beautiful tree her entire extended family enjoys every year as they feast on a full Irish breakfast—eggs, sausage, rashers, tomatoes, black pudding, tea, and scones—on Christmas morning. "Top o' the Christmas mornin' to you!"

You, too, can do up a Family Tree. All you need is a love of family—and your own kinship secrets of the past.

BARBIE DOES CHRISTMAS

Every thirty seconds, someone buys a Barbie doll—and that's just those bought for little girls. Grown-up girls love Barbie, too, which is why there are some 100,000 avid collectors willing to shell out as much as $1,000 a year on Barbie paraphernalia. Lucky for them—and your favorite Barbie fan—there are lots of Barbie Christmas decorations on the market. You'll find Barbie Christmas garlands, Barbie Christmas stockings, Barbie Christmas dolls, and Barbie Christmas ornaments in the shape of classic Barbie accessories such as handbags, makeup kits, sunglasses, and cell phones. What's more, not only can you outfit your house in Christmas Barbie, you can outfit Barbie's Dream House as well by stocking up on all the miniature Barbie Christmas goodies. Do it right, and you can have a real Barbie Christmas—just make sure Ken gets her a nice gift!

GEEK CHRISTMAS #1

If you're a geek, or if you're in love with a geek, then you may have trouble pulling your dork away from the computer long enough to trim the tree. If this is true for you, then borrow a trick from our friend Lacey from Silicon Valley, who bribes her cute but nerdy boyfriend, Hal, into celebrating Christmas by declaring it an official High-Tech Holiday. With a little push from Lacey, Hal's really into it now; he's proud of the Christmas tree, which is totally tricked out with green circuit boards in the shapes of bells, trees, stars, hearts, cell phones, and digital cameras. The light system is amazing; we'd tell you how he does it but we'd have to kill you. Or at least hack into your computer.

Merry Christmas to George Lucas

In Christmas of 2008, sales of Star Wars toys and products were the strongest they'd been in some thirty years—raking in more than $450 million.

GEEK CHRISTMAS #2:
STAR WARS EDITION

There's no stopping the dyed-in-the-Wookiee-wool Star Wars fan. And with so much stuff available for a Star Wars Christmas, all it takes is a little imagination to go Ewok-wild. (We have a friend, who shall remain nameless, from Las Vegas for whom Christmas vacation is one long Star Wars movie marathon, complete with costumes.) On the Internet you can find official Star Wars Christmas snow globes, Christmas stockings, ornaments, and more. Our favorites: M&M's Amidala figurine featuring the queen in royal regalia and the candy-coated Princess Padme. May the Yuletide Force be with you.

Christmas Comes to the White House

Franklin Pierce brought the first Christmas tree to the White House in 1853.

NAME-YOUR-OBSESSION CHRISTMAS TREE

If you can name a theme, you can decorate around that theme. A quick online search and you'll find ornaments in the shape of mermaids, big foot, dinosaurs, Elvis, cups of cappuccino or espresso with tags so you know what the hell they are, even s'mores—a graham cracker platform topped with chocolate and two marshmallows wearing sports uniforms (basketball, soccer, or football). So if you want it, you can have it. All you need is a predilection for the weird and a credit card, and you're good to go.

Feminine Hygiene Christmas

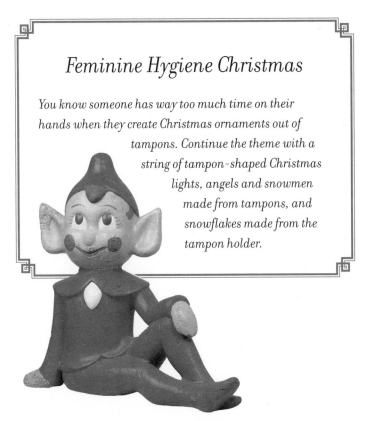

You know someone has way too much time on their hands when they create Christmas ornaments out of tampons. Continue the theme with a string of tampon-shaped Christmas lights, angels and snowmen made from tampons, and snowflakes made from the tampon holder.

WREATHED IN SPRING

Wreaths have long been symbols of success, though the kind of success varied according to its wearer. The ancient Persians wore wreaths known as diadems as headbands to indicate prestige and wealth. The ancient Pagans decorated their homes with evergreen wreaths as a promise of spring during the winter solstice (spring being a sign of success of a different kind—proof that they'd survived yet another winter). The Greeks crowned their Olympic champions with wreaths of laurel—which the athletes later would hang on the walls of their homes as trophies. The pre-Christian Germanic people used evergreen wreaths lit by candles during the winter—a tradition that the medieval Christians adapted into the Advent wreath, with which they prepared for the coming of the baby Jesus. Whatever the wreath's origin, these days placing a Christmas wreath on your front door is a sign that Christmas is coming—and you'd better get busy.

The Sweet Smell of Rosemary

During the Middle Ages, people would spread fresh rosemary on their floors at Christmas in the hope that the fragrant smell would fill the house. Christians believed that rosemary had gained its sweet fragrance when Mary laid baby Jesus's garments on its branches. They also thought it had the power to ward off evil spirits.

WREATHS OF GLORY FOR
FALLEN SOLDIERS

In 1992, Maine resident Morrill Worcester had a surplus of wreaths in his holiday decorating business and decided to drive them to Washington, D.C., to lay them on gravesites in Arlington National Cemetery. It quickly became a tradition and now members of the armed forces, civil air patrol, veterans of foreign wars, and several civilians gather annually to help Mr. Worcester lay wreaths on all 5,000 graves, including the Tomb of the Unknowns.

THE POINSETTIA COMES TO AMERICA

Every year Americans spend $220 million on poinsettias. Poinsettias originated in Central and South America, where they were revered by the ancient Aztec peoples and were later used to decorate during Christmas. To Christians, their red petals represent the blood shed for human redemption and their green leaves show the promise of new life and rebirth.

In 1824, the American ambassador to Mexico, Joel Poinsett, attended church service on Christmas Eve and fell in love with the bright red flowers decorating the church altar. When he returned to America, he brought seeds and shared the plants with local churches to decorate for Christmas celebrations. People began referring to them as Poinsett's plants, or poinsettias. Popular worldwide today, poinsettias are now the most popular flowering potted plant in the United States.

THE MAGIC OF MISTLETOE

Mistletoe has long been considered a mysterious, magical plant. A parasitic plant that grows on trees, it is a sacred staple in European folklore, believed to promote life, enhance fertility, and even serve as an aphrodisiac. The druids, members of a pagan religious order in ancient Gaul, Britain, and Ireland, held the mistletoe in such reverence that if enemies happened to meet under it in the forest, a truce was declared for the day. They hung mistletoe over the door to ward off darkness and to invite happiness. When the Yule season approached, the prince of the druids used a golden sickle to cut down mistletoe from the sacred oaks; he then distributed the mistletoe to the people, who believed it possessed powers to protect against sickness and evil.

The druids were not alone in their regard for this enchanted plant. There are a number of supernatural beliefs about mistletoe, including the following.

Mistletoe is also believed to

- Keep goblins away from infants, if placed in their crib.
- Protect households from thunder and lightning.
- Protect the entire herd for the year, if given to the first cow giving birth after New Year's.
- Heal disease and render poison harmless.
- Protect your house from witchcraft and ghosts.

THE MISTLETOE MYTH

According to Scandinavian pagan mythology, mistletoe was the sacred plant of Frigga, the goddess of love and the mother of Balder, the god of the summer sun. When Balder had a dream of death, his mother begged air, fire, water, earth, and every animal and plant to promise that no harm would come to her son. Unfortunately, Loki, the god of evil, noticed that Frigga had overlooked mistletoe in her quest to keep her son safe. Loki used mistletoe to construct an arrow tip and gave it to Hoder, the blind god of winter. When Hoder used the arrow tip to strike Balder dead, the sky paled and all things in earth and heaven wept for the god of the summer sun. For three days Frigga and the elements struggled to bring Balder back to life. When Frigga finally restored him, her tears turned into the pearly white berries on the mistletoe plant. Happy that her son had been saved, Frigga kissed everyone who passed beneath the tree on which the mistletoe grew. Thereafter, whoever stood under the humble mistletoe would be safe from harm and receive only a kiss, a token of love.

Shoes and Socks, Please

Shoes and socks play an important role at Christmas. From stockings hung by the chimney with care to wooden shoes left by the door, these (often smelly) everyday items have been the vessels of Christmas goodies for centuries.

IT'S A SHOE THING

All over the world, children expect their shoes to be filled with treats, mostly thanks to the legends surrounding St. Nicholas. The traditions vary according to their place of origin:

- In France, children place their shoes by the fireplace, a tradition dating back to when children wore wooden peasant shoes.

- In Holland, children fill their shoes with hay and a carrot for the horse of Sinterklaas.

- In Hungary, children shine their shoes before putting them near the door or a windowsill.

- Italian children leave their shoes out the night before Epiphany, January 5, for La Befana, the good witch.

HANG 'EM HIGH

The first mention of Christmas stockings being hung from or near a chimney came in the classic *'Twas the Night Before Christmas*, in which illustrator Thomas Nast and writer Clement Moore immortalized the stockings "hung by the chimney with care, in hopes that St. Nicholas soon would be there." The story, first known as "A Visit from St. Nicholas," quickly caught on—and with it the custom of hanging Christmas stockings. Children all over the world continue the tradition today.

Do They Have Camels in Puerto Rico?

In Puerto Rico, children put greens and flowers in small boxes and place them under their beds for the camels of the Three Kings.

Chapter Four
'TIS BETTER TO GIVE . . .

Or Why Beauty Is in the Eye of the Gift Giver

The average American family spends between $600 and $800 on Christmas gifts every year. That's a lot of money on ties, reindeer sweaters, and soon-to-be-obsolete gadgets and gizmos. But with typical Yankee ingenuity, many Americans have created gift-giving guidelines and shopping rules and rituals that defy the norm. From the sublime to the ridiculous, these practices are as varied as their creators—and as unique.

THE FIFTY-FIFTY CHRISTMAS

If you're thinking of a way to make your holiday season more meaningful, consider taking at least half of your usual seasonal expenditures and giving those funds to those less fortunate. That's what the Lovelace family of California does. Every year they sit down with their Christmas budget and decide what they really want, what they can cut out, and what they can give to those who need it most. They're creative about it, taking such cost-effective measures as

- Sending out holiday e-mails, wishing friends and family happy holidays and telling them that they're forgoing Christmas cards this year and donating the savings to charity

- Involving the kids, who trim their own wish lists and help buy toys for disadvantaged children with the difference
- Deciding as a family how to appropriate the money

Some years they adopt a local family; other years they've visited shelters, hospital wards, and assisted living homes, laden with toys and gifts for all. The Lovelaces say that this approach reminds them about the true meaning of Christmas every year—and has brought them closer together as a family.

You, too, can dedicate half—or all!—of your holiday budget to such a charitable cause. You'll be glad you did—and, like the Lovelaces, find that every year will be a Christmas to remember.

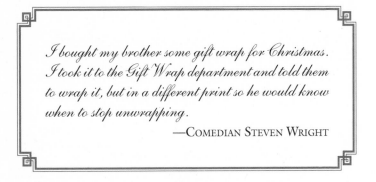

I bought my brother some gift wrap for Christmas. I took it to the Gift Wrap department and told them to wrap it, but in a different print so he would know when to stop unwrapping.

—COMEDIAN STEVEN WRIGHT

THE SOCKS WERE HUNG BY THE CHIMNEY WITH CARE

You've heard of filling the stockings of bad little boys and girls with coal. But few have heard of Mrs. Johnson's stocking-stuffing ritual. Mrs. Johnson from Pittsburgh has six sons. That's a lot of athletic socks. Dirty athletic socks. So every year she stuffs her boys' stockings with new socks. The first year she did it as a joke, but the boys got such a kick out of it—and she was so thrilled to start the new year off right by ditching all their ratty old socks in favor of their new Christmas socks—that she continued to stuff those stockings with socks year after year. If you've got boys—and you're short on coal—you might appropriate Mrs. Johnson's Sock It to 'Em Stocking Stuffer Ritual.

Top Ten Worst Stocking Stuffers

Hedge funds	*Fruitcake*
Coal	*Grooming tools*
Argyle socks	*Christmas Carol CDs*
Nuts	*Soap*
Fruit	*Underwear*

YANKEE SWAP FROM HELL

In New England, the Yankee Swap is a time-honored tradition that supposedly dates back to the Civil War. Lore has it that the Northerners offered to swap some of their prisoners with some of the Confederates' prisoners—and the so-called Yankee Swap was born. Nearly 150 years later, in offices all over America, countless people buy $10 gifts, wrap them up, pull a number from a hat, and begin the pseudo-bonding ritual of swapping gifts. This saves them buying presents for all of their colleagues—and limits their Christmas liability to only ten bucks. But if you really want to do the Yankee Swap right, you need to observe the original stipulation: Everyone who participates brings not a new gift purchased for the event, but something from home that they already have. This is re-gifting on a whole new level; apparently the ever-frugal Yankees were the original re-gifters.

If you really want to up the ante on your Yankee Swap, you can add another stipulation, the one used by a certain family from Maine that will remain nameless: When choosing something from home to bring to the swap, make it something terrible. The uglier and less desirable the "gift," the better. Now the intent of this holiday exercise becomes not to swap for the best present, but rather to swap to avoid the worst. When the victim of your Yankee Swap from Hell ends up with that pee-colored tie your mother-in-law knitted you last year, just smile sweetly and say, "Merry Christmas!"

POINT OF NO RETURN

Some forty million Americans return their Christmas presents every year—but not the Prue household in southern Nevada. Aurea, the seventy-three-year-old matriarch of the Prue clan, has long imposed a "no return" rule in regard to gifts. The idea is *not* to buy whatever strikes your fancy or suits your pocketbook, but rather to think long and hard about each person on your shopping list, and determine the perfect gift for everyone. Do this, and there's no reason for the recipients of your gifts to return them.

This puts the pressure on the giver, which, according to Aurea, is where it should be. Why give a gift that's inappropriate, unsuitable, or unwanted? What's the point in that? Christmas is the time to show your love and appreciation for the people you care most about—that's why we give gifts, after all. This is Gift Giving Without a Net, for hard-core shoppers and/or creative geniuses only. Good luck with that.

Christmas Gifts Most Likely to Be Returned

Duplicate gifts

Video games

CDs

Shoes

Socks

Movies

Clothes

Housewares

Age-inappropriate toys

Just plain ugly stuff

SHOP 'TIL YOU DROP

For some people, Christmas doesn't really happen until December 26. If your idea of a good time is a little retail therapy, then the Day-After holiday is the one you should celebrate. One Dallas family we know is honest enough to admit that they don't attach any religious, sentimental, or familial meaning to the holiday season. For them, conspicuous consumers all, the best part of Christmas is the sales that hit the stores once it's over. So every year they give each other cash on Christmas—and spend the day planning their shopping strategies for December 26.

Over the years, they've learned all the tricks to getting the best deals on what is traditionally one of the busiest days in retail. First, they decide what they most want, and prioritize accordingly. Second, because they've got only cash to spend—rather than presents to return—they avoid the returns traffic, which is the factor that accounts for the lion's share of the crowds. Third, they go through all the ads leading up to this fateful day, and supplement that with online research, so they know where and when to go to really capitalize on all the best, heaviest discounting. Fourth, they make pit stops every few hours for breakfast, lunch, and dinner—to keep their energy and their spirits up. When they finally head home after a long day of shopping, they bliss out over rum-spiked eggnog (sparkling cider for the kids) and hold a Shopping Show-and-Tell and Fashion Show, in which they parade all their new clothes, toys, and luxuries.

If you're all about getting rather than giving, you too, can indulge your inner sport shopper every year. Just be sure to wear comfortable shoes when you hit the mall for your shopping marathon!

THE UGLY CHRISTMAS SWEATER CONTEST

Everyone has an ugly holiday sweater: a Christmas tree sweatshirt that lights up; a Santa Suit sweater complete with fur trim and a bowl full of jelly; a partridge-in-a-pear-tree vest that sings "The Twelve Days of Christmas" when you push its beak. These ho-ho-ho garments have become ubiquitous, if homely, symbols of the holiday season—and sooner or later, you'll be wearing one. Even movie stars wear them: Remember Colin Firth as Mr. Darcy in the hideous reindeer sweater in *Bridget Jones's Diary*?

At the Carr cousins' Christmas in Maine, the wearing of ugly Yuletide pullovers has become a formal competition. On the last Sunday of Advent, all of the Carr cousins gather at Aunt Susie's house for the annual gift exchange and the Ugly Christmas Sweater Contest. Everyone participates, from the newborn babes to the great-grandparents. The kids get individual presents, but the adults each contribute $10 to the contest kitty, all of which goes to the Grand Prize Winner. Everyone takes part in the judging, which is done by secret ballot. The Ugly Christmas Sweater Contest is the highlight of the Carr cousins' Christmas—you might try it with your cousins as well!

THE CHRISTMAS GIFT BOX

We have Oprah to thank for this one. On one of her Christmas shows she told a story about one of the most cherished gifts she'd ever received. "A few years ago at my 50th Birthday luncheon, my friends wrote me heartfelt notes that they then placed inside this silver box," Oprah says. "The words from your heart mean more to people than anything you can buy." Millions of Americans saw that show, and doubtless many of them chose to re-create the ritual within their own families.

One such family, the Oldhams, are scattered to the far corners of the world most of the year, but every Christmas they come from East and West, Europe and South America, to enjoy a multicultural holiday together in Las Vegas. The matriarch of the family, an Oprah fan, saw the show and had silver boxes engraved for every member of the family, each personalized with the recipient's name. Before distributing the boxes, she handed out cards to everyone, and had them write short notes about one another. She made it into a game, everyone guessing who wrote what about whom. After much love and laughter, they each received their silver boxes, which would hold the cards. "It is hard to be so far away from each other so much of the time," she told them. "But now when we miss each other, we can open our boxes, and read our cards, and hold each other in our hearts."

THE TRIP THAT KEEPS ON GIVING

Every year, Monica and Eric from Washington State stuff their backpacks with jeans, T-shirts, and toys for disadvantaged tots. The week before Christmas, they board a plane for Africa. Several planes, trains, boats, and buses later, they arrive at a village in South Africa, where they distribute the toys, jeans, and T-shirts to the children there. They've been going there for a decade now—the ten happiest holidays of their lives. They've been made honorary citizens of the town, and are accepted as fixtures every December. They come home content with what they can give, and grateful for what they have. You, too, can adopt a village for Christmas. And you don't have to travel to another continent if you don't want to. Every state in the union has hamlets, towns, and neighborhoods where children go without new clothes and toys every Christmas. Make a trip to that place every year, and you too will take a trip that keeps on giving.

HOLIDAY HANSON

When native Bostonian Jennifer Brighton married native New Yorker Harry Hanson, she had no idea that her holidays would change forever. It wasn't that Harry was Jewish, and didn't believe in celebrating Christmas; it was that Harry had a "bah, humbug" attitude about all holidays. He didn't celebrate birthdays, Valentine's Day, Mother's Day, Father's Day, Christmas, or even Hanukkah. Harry enjoyed American holidays involving picnics or champagne-soaked feasts, but when it came to birthdays or gift-giving holidays, Harry was, well, an old-fashioned grumpy, stingy grinch. Even though it drove poor Jennifer crazy, over the years she adjusted, opting to observe her favorite holidays with people who did decorate for Christmas and did exchange gifts. Although he was sweet in every other way, Harry remained obstinate and never caved in. Eventually, it became such a joke among their friends that they dubbed him "Holiday Hanson" and ribbed him on every occasion. And good ole Harry just smiled and wore his moniker proudly. Not to be outdone, Jennifer began her own holiday tradition—she buys whatever she wants, wraps it in fancy paper, gifts it to herself, opens it in front of Harry, and exclaims, "Harry, you shouldn't have!"

GIFT-GIVING 101

It's amazing how many people have virtually no capacity whatsoever for successful gift giving. Every present they give is eventually returned—with or without their knowledge. And it is a truth universally acknowledged (by wives) that most of these gift-challenged people are husbands. If you're one of the wives who's received such romantic, thoughtful gifts as a chain saw, tickets to a monster truck rally, or fake diamonds, then you know what we're saying. You may have thought you were doomed to receive cheap perfume and fly-fishing waders for the rest of your married Christmases—but it doesn't have to be that way. All you need to do is give your guy a little course in presents we like to call Gift-Giving 101. And here's the best part: You can train your man to give great gifts without his even knowing.

That's what Jane from Boston did, when presented with one too many Precious Moments statues from her hubby, Mike. She complained to her mother, who recommended a fail-proof strategy that she swore—okay she didn't swear, she never swears—would work on any man. Mom instructed Jane to find a picture in a magazine that represented *exactly* what she wanted for Christmas, and put it on the refrigerator door. Jane did as her mother advised and found a lovely ad for the perfect strand of pearls, and attached it with Red Sox magnets to the fridge door at eye level. It'll have a subliminal effect, her mother promised her. That said, subliminal messages always need a little conscious help. So two weeks before Christmas, Jane's mother took Mike aside and said, "I saw a string of pearls just like the ones in that photo on your fridge. Would you like me to pick them up for you for Jane for Christmas?" Mike handed over the money for the pearls to Mom, Mom handed over the pearls to Mike, and on Christmas Day, Jane opened the best present she'd ever gotten from Mike, the love of her life.

If the love of your life suffers from gift-giving blindness, then open his eyes by putting your own four-color advertisement up on the fridge. Just remind your mother to check in with your man a couple of weeks before Christmas to bring it home for you.

The Ethic of Reciprocity

Otherwise known as the Golden Rule, this is the code considered by many to be the basis of human rights. It is best known today as, "Do unto others as you would have them do unto you." You can apply this to your gift giving as well. For those few who give you gifts that are truly thoughtful, and desired by you, return the favor. For those who give you fruitcake . . . well, fruitcake them right back.

THE GOLDEN RULE OF GIVING

For every couple, Christmas can be a make-or-break time. The pressure is on to get your spouse the perfect present, a present that somehow communicates your undying love and support 'til death do you part—each and every year until such time. Just like in the classic O'Henry story "The Gift of the Magi."

But for many couples, life is not an O'Henry story. Some couples resign themselves to a lifetime of disappointment (and secret resentment); some dismiss the entire idea out of hand, if only in self-defense. They say "Christmas is for the kids" or "There's no point in trying; she always returns what I get her" or "How many ties can one guy wear, anyway?" Cheryl and Bob from Raleigh have been there. After one particularly miserable Christmas, they hit upon a gift-giving strategy that never fails to please them both. In a splendid twist on "The Gift of the Magi" story, they each give the other exactly what the other wants. How do they accomplish this seemingly impossible task year in and year out? Simple: Cheryl gives Bob the present *she* most wants, and he gives her the present *he* most wants. Then they swap gifts—and everybody's happy!

CHOOSE YOUR OWN CHRISTMAS ADVENTURE

You've read those Choose Your Own Adventure kids' books, haven't you? Well, you can choose your own Christmas adventure for you and your loved ones—and give your family a gift they'll remember for the rest of their lives. The Boswells from Ohio love to travel—and when they had children, they were determined to keep on traveling, kids in tow. So they spend Christmas vacation on the road, as a family. They keep gift giving to a minimum, as these holiday trips are the gift they give the whole family, and travel to exotic places both at home and abroad. They've explored the volcanoes of Hawaii on the Big Island, gone swimming with the dolphins in Florida, and learned to ski in Vermont. They've watched monkeys swing from the trees in Costa Rica, climbed the 704 visitors' steps of the Eiffel Tower, and played on the beaches of Mallorca. Every year it's a trip of a lifetime—and one for the family album. You can choose your own adventure for Christmas, too. All you need is a globe and a pin—just spin the orb, stick in the pin, and off you go. Bon Voyage!

IT'S A TAROT PARTY!

Every new year brings with it the promise of better things to come. We read our horoscopes, make resolutions, start diets, and end relationships—anything and everything to get the new year off to a good start. We're obsessed with trying to read—and influence—our own futures.

Paula's been reading tarot cards for years. She's good at it—but she doesn't do it professionally: just for friends and family. Every New Year's Day, Paula invites all her best girl-friends to her house for an overnight pizza party. They drink wine and eat pizza, then Paula lights the candles, pulls out the tarot cards, and does a special tarot reading for each guest. She uses a tarot spread that's perfect for the new year, and uses it to predict the highs and lows of each woman's career, relation-ships, and more for the coming year. It's her annual holiday gift to them—and they love it!

Tarot Divination

The tarot dates back to the fifteenth century in Italy. Originally believed to be used to play a game similar to bridge, these decks of cards are now used primarily for divination.

THE EX FACTOR

You're divorced, but you had kids together, and so every year you're faced with the question: Am I big enough to spend good money on someone I never want to see again, but am forced to see every time we exchange the kids, just so I look like a good person? The short answer is: Yes. Even if you got robbed blind. Even if you never get a dime or pay out exor-bitant child support and alimony. Why? Because your kids are watching you. So, do it this way: Take your kids to buy your ex something nice for the holidays every year. Help them wrap it up beautifully, and have them present it when they're at the ex's house over the holidays. Your ex will know where it really came from—and so will your kids. And years later when they ask, "Why do you always do this even though Mom/Dad never reciprocates?" you can smile sweetly, as Joan from Santa Barbara does every year, and say, "Because I want you to grow up to be the kind of people who always remember their mother/father at Christmas."

Top Ten Gifts to Give Your Ex for Christmas (from You)

Divorce papers

Custody of the teenagers

Pictures of you with your ex's best friend

Pictures of your ex's lover with someone else

A court order for back child support

An invitation to your wedding

Half your worthless 401(k)

A subscription to Match.com

The name of a good therapist

A bus ticket out of town

PLAYING SANTA

Playing Santa is a time-honored tradition in many families. Usually this means dressing up as jolly old St. Nick and passing out gifts to all the children at the annual holiday get-together. But for some, playing Santa is a little less conventional—and a lot more fun. Ted and Alice from Providence indulge in this Yuletide role-playing every year. Ted puts on the red suit, and Alice fills the sack full of toys for their favorite charity. Together they drop off the gifts, and then Santa drops Alice off at their apartment. While Alice slips into something more comfortable, and sets out milk and cookies for Santa, Santa refills his sack— this time with champagne and Chinese food. By the time he gets home, Alice has just settled down for a long winter's nap. But she doesn't get much sleep.

If you've always had a thing for red suits, you might try playing Santa this year yourself. Just don't forget the milk and cookies.

COLD, HARD CHRISTMAS CASH

"When in doubt, give cash"—that's the motto of the Sellers family from New Jersey. Rather than spend endless hours, days, and weeks shopping, shopping and wrapping, shopping and wrapping and shipping, the Jacksons just present each other with the only thing they know they really want: money. Money is always the right color, the right size, the right style.

The Sellers start their Christmas cash program early—at birth. The children receive a dollar for every year of their age for each of the twelve days of Christmas. By the time they are eighteen, they've topped out at a whopping $216! The grown-ups set their own fiscal limits, based on financial considerations and personal preferences. Do the math: This could work for you, too.

NO-NAME CHRISTMAS

They say that there are two kinds of giving. The first is when you give to someone, and the recipient knows you are the giver. The second is when you give to someone, but remain anonymous. This is a higher form of giving—what the Morrisons from Portland, Oregon, call No-Name Giving. Every year the Morrisons take stock of their finances, and decide how much they can give away. Then they keep their eyes and ears open, looking for a worthy recipient who needs help but has nowhere to turn. Their research—checking with local newspapers, hospitals, and clergy—helps them identify people who especially need help. Over the years they've anonymously presented a new motorized wheelchair to a terminally ill child, paid the rent for a family whose single mother had just lost her job, and funded a playground for a local day-care center. The monetary value of the gifts may vary from year to year based on the Morrisons' financial status, but one thing remains constant: What they give they give as the No Namers. It's one family secret they're all secretly proud of.

The trick to No-Name Giving is being able to work together—and then keep your mouth shut. This may be a tall order for many families, so keep that in mind as you decide whether to try this with your loved ones.

SECRET SANTA

If you think Secret Santas are just for kids, think again. Secret Santa is a great way to hit on girls—and guys. Say you have a crush on the redhead in the cubicle down the pod from yours. Red doesn't seem to know you're even alive, but you can use the spirit of the season to seduce the object of your interest. Start a week before the office Christmas party. Observe Red's patterns of coming and going (which you may already have noted, if your crush is bordering on stalking). Go out and buy seven gifts, one for each day of the week. The gifts should be appropriate for the office, but slightly more personal. (Even if

---

Secret Santa Gifts for Her

Bottle of her favorite wine

Novel by her favorite author

DVD of her favorite romantic comedy

Candle infused with her favorite scent

Fresh bouquet of her favorite flowers

A perfect single serving of her favorite dessert

Tickets to a theater/opera/event she'd love

---

you really are a stalker, you don't want Red to know it.) For example, a bottle of wine is a classic gift. You know that Red really prefers red wine, naturally, particularly cabernets from Kendall Jackson. Indulge Red. Once you've found seven such presents, plant one in her cubicle each day when there's no one around to see you do it. This may mean bribing the security guard—whatever works. On the last day, the day of the Christmas party, leave a note with the last present asking Red to meet you at a bar for a nightcap after the party. We know a guy who found his wife this way. And every year on the anniversary of that fateful Christmas party where he declared himself, they share a bottle of Kendall Jackson cabernet.

Secret Santa Gifts for Him

Six pack from his favorite microbrewery

Biography of his favorite hero

DVD of his favorite action flick

Concert T-shirt from his favorite band

Cool new case for his iPod/BlackBerry/whatever

A homemade apple pie

Tickets to a game/concert/event he'd love

THE ALL-AMERICAN GIFT SWAP

Each year we all receive gifts that defy explanation: the singing fish wall plaque, the Scooby Doo Chia Pet, the fruitcake that doubles as a doorstop. If not absolutely ridiculous, the gifts can be simply inappropriate: the handsaw for the uptown girl, the comic-book tie for the man in a Brooks Brothers suit, the ten-gallon cowboy hat for the inveterate New Yorker. And all the wives on earth have at least one story about the wildly weird gifts they've gotten from clueless husbands over the years. In suburban California, there's a group of housewives desperate to get rid of the presents they don't want—and don't want to bother returning, either.

So rather than face the nightmare crowds at the mall on December 26 to stand in endless lines to return their unwanted gifts, they all gather at someone's house for a post-Christmas brunch and gift swap. Everyone brings the gifts they don't want—the sweaters in unflattering colors, the age-inappropriate toys, the too-small lingerie, etc.—and display them. That's when the horse trading begins—fueled by pitchers of mimosas and a playful competitive spirit. And because one girl's fashion don't is another girl's fashion do, everyone ends up with something they like. Still, there are usually at least some gifts nobody wants; these are donated to charity. As a parting shot, the women vote on the Worst Gift of the Year. Whoever wins this dubious honor has to host the party next year.

THE TWELVE DAYS OF CHRISTMAS

Christmas doesn't have to be the end all and be all of the holiday season. If you want to prolong the joys of this special season, you can reinvent the tradition of the Twelve Days of Christmas—just as Uncle Jim from Indiana has always done. Uncle Jim loves Christmas. In fact, he loves it so much that he always takes the entire month of December off, from December 1 all the way up to January 6. He spends the weeks before Christmas planning and preparing for the Twelve Days of Christmas. He strings up lights around the house and sets up elaborate decorations in the yard. He helps his wife trim the tree and decorate the inside of their home. He makes gingerbread houses and evergreen wreaths and wooden ornaments. He plays Santa for the local kindergarten classes, sings in the church Christmas choir, and shops for the perfect presents for his loved ones. He makes pots and pots of his special three-alarm Christmas chili, bakes a dozen apple pies, and helps his wife wrap all the gifts. Once Christmas arrives, everything is ready—and Uncle Jim opens his doors. Anyone can drop by—and everyone does. Uncle Jim presides over the next twelve days—the Twelve Days of Christmas—a whirlwind of food, friends, and family.

You don't have to use all your vacation every year for Christmas—but you might want to try taking off the Twelve Days of Christmas. As Uncle Jim always says, there's no point in doing all that prep work for just Christmas Day. Enjoy all Twelve Days of Christmas—and you'll be glad you did.

MAKE IT YOURSELF

Back in the Dark Ages, long before credit card debt and online shopping, people made each other presents for Christmas—with their own hands. They knitted scarves and whittled whistles and made dolls out of corn husks. They baked cookies and made fruitcakes and spooned apple butter into Bell jars. They dried flowers and painted pictures and threw pots. All of which made swell Christmas presents. Well, except maybe the fruitcake. The good news is that you, too, can turn the tables on our overly commercialized twenty-first-century holiday and declare a Make It Yourself Christmas for you and yours.

The Carringtons of Utah make presents for their loved ones every year. Mr. Carrington is a gifted photographer whose creative photographic portraits of friends and family are highly prized by their lucky recipients. He even fashions the frames out of local walnut. Mrs. Carrington is an accomplished candy maker whose hand-dipped chocolates are on everyone's wish list. Even the Carrington kids get into the act. Under the watchful eye of their handy parents, they've made all kinds of gifts—from candles and potpourri to crocheted afghans and hand-built shelves. You can make your gift giving just as special. Agree as a family to make your presents this year—and put your talents and hobbies to work. Write a song for your spouse, plant an herb garden for your mother, carve a wooden toy for your child. No one really needs another (store-bought) sweater—give a one-of-a-kind gift you've made yourself. You'll be glad you did.

ALMOST HOMEMADE

If the story about the Make-It-Yourself Carringtons makes you sweat, relax. Even if you find yourself thoroughly ensconced in a family full of talented craftspeople when you don't know a paint brush from a hair brush or a crochet hook from a fish hook or a jigsaw from a jigsaw puzzle, don't panic. You can fake it by mastering the (oh-so-easy) art of Almost Homemade. There are a number of sneaky ways you can "create" gifts for your friends and family without lifting a finger.

The easiest way: Simply buy something homemade and swap out the label for one of your own (you can order these online from *www.namemaker.com*). The trick to this strategy is not to go too upscale with the gift, lest you engender suspicion upon the part of the recipient. For example, if you want to give a hand-knitted sweater, pick one up at your local crafts fair— rather than spending a small fortune on a fisherman's sweater knit by a grandmother in a remote Irish fishing village. The same goes for "your" special apple butter, crocheted doilies, or carpentry work. If anyone asks you for your trade secrets, just smile sweetly and say, "I could never reveal the secret ingredient/stitch/pattern endowed to me by my father/grandfather/person the recipient has never heard of."

If such duplicity strikes you as decidedly un-Christmas, then there are a couple of other strategies you can try. One: Instead of giving gifts you made, give your crafty loved ones a basket full of the most exclusive tools, materials, and instruction pertaining to *their* craft/hobby/art form. Think skeins of hand-dyed, hand-spun wool for the knitter in your life, a new saw for the carpenter, a new easel for the painter. Two: Just fess up to the fact that you're not at all crafty, and go ahead and give that fisherman's sweater knit by a grandmother in a remote fishing village. Leave the original label in, and proclaim loudly as you present the gift, "My greatest talent is recognizing the talent of others."

RESOLUTIONS TO PARTY BY

New Year's resolutions are easy to make—and hard to keep. You may even find yourself making the same resolutions over and over again every year. This is the year I'm going to stop smoking, or take up running, or give up fast food, you say. But by the time mid-January comes around, you're usually back on the couch sneaking cigs between Big Macs. This year can be differ-

Most Boring New Year's Resolutions

Quit smoking.

Get a divorce.

Quit drinking.

Make a budget and stick to it.

Get organized.

Go on a diet.

Get out of debt.

Go to the gym.

ent. Whatever you resolve to do, throw a party to announce your resolution, and invite lots of like-minded pals. Resolve to honor your collective resolution together—and keep one another on track. That's what Judy from New Orleans did. Frustrated by her inability to write that novel she's always planned to write, Judy threw a New Year's party, and invited all the other frustrated writers she knew. Together they resolved to write more in the year to come, and they founded a writer's group that very night. Every week thereafter they met to read and discuss their work. Thanks to the group's determination and encouragement, Judy finished her first novel—and has gone on to write a second. You too can meet all of your goals—with a little help from your friends. Plan your Resolutions Party today!

Most Un-boring New Year's Resolutions

Have an affair.

Have an affair with someone famous.

Go on vacation.

Quit your job.

Move to Paris.

Learn to tango.

Buy a new wardrobe.

Have more sex/chocolate/champagne.

NEW YEAR, NEW YOU

Every January bookstores from sea to shining sea feature New Year, New You promotions. They put out tables and end caps of books dedicated to the all-American guiding principle of self-improvement. Books that tell you how to get a date, find a mate, lose weight, get fit, stop drinking, give up smoking, land a new job, change careers, get rich quick, achieve enlightenment, and on and on. You can plan your own New Year, New You promotion. Buy a book, join a support group. Or better yet, book yourself into an appropriate event during the holidays to jump-start your transformation. Spend a week at a spa; check yourself into a detox program; indulge in a yoga retreat. If your friends and family complain about your going away and/or doing something for yourself instead of them, ignore them. And remind them that this way you'll become a better person—and that's a gift to everyone you love, yourself included!

A COUPLE'S CHRISTMAS

Sometimes all you really want for Christmas is some alone time with your partner. If this is how you feel, take a cue from a very devoted Cincinnati couple we'll call the Carlsons. They dump all their familial obligations and check themselves into a suite at a four-star hotel every Christmas Eve. Once happily ensconced in their room, they turn off their cell phones and BlackBerries, unplug their computers, and order room service. They slip into their pajamas, and take full advantage of the king-size bed, hot tub, and minibar. While the rest of the world is running around picking up last-minute gifts, wrapping overpriced presents no one really wants, and heading over to Grandma's for another rubber-turkey dinner, the Carlsons are wrapped happily in each other's arms, sipping champagne, dining on chateaubriand, and watching movies on the 60-inch flat-screen TV. They have the time of their lives—then sleep in. They don't leave the room until check-out time at noon the next day—Christmas Day. On their way home, they drop by Mom's house for Christmas dinner. They're always the happiest, most relaxed people there. You can do the same thing—all you need is your partner and a commitment to tuning out all Christmas chaos for a full twenty-four hours.

MERRY CHRISTMAS TO ME

Okay, so you're alone again on Christmas. Just like millions of other Americans. But you don't have to wallow in self-pity. Instead of spending the day drinking too much, eating too much, and watching *It's a Wonderful Life* over and over again, you can have a truly special Christmas for One. That's what Sarah M. from Connecticut does every year. A childless widow, Sarah has mastered the art of spending Christmas alone. She treats the holiday as a gift to herself, an annual indulgence in all things Sarah, and devotes the entire day to herself. She buys herself the perfect present, the present no one else in the world knows her well enough to choose for her. One year it was a first edition of a much-loved novel; another year it was a turquoise and silver ring made by a much-admired local artist. She dons her favorite silk pajamas, eats her favorite foods, and reads her favorite magazines. Whatever she feels like doing—sleeping in, dancing in her underwear, writing in her journal—she does. Whatever she doesn't feel like doing, she doesn't. You can adopt this same attitude—and turn your forlorn sorrow into a celebratory solitude. Make Christmas all about you—because you're worth it!

ON-THE-ROAD CHRISTMAS

If you don't want to be home for Christmas, hit the road. Pack a weekend bag, stick a pin in a local map, and take off for parts unknown. Stick to the back roads, and explore the country side of Christmas. You can plan ahead and book a room at some off-the-beaten-path motel, or pitch a tent in a park. Harry and Rachel from Las Vegas have done this every year they've been together—nearly a decade of on-the-road Christmases. They've traveled down Route 66, wound round Big Sur on Highway 1, and driven the Loneliest Highway in America (Route 50 in Nevada). They've stayed in teepees, log cabins, and quaint inns. They've bunked in barracks, slept in sleeping bags under the stars, and even spent one night in a monastery. Every Christmas is an adventure—and proof that sometimes the best way to spend Christmas is in your own Santa sleigh—on wheels.

WINNERS-TAKE-ALL CHRISTMAS

If you like to gamble, you'll love this gifting ritual. Instead of handing out presents, gambling givers put their trust in the lottery. One Las Vegas family we know has abandoned traditional gift giving altogether, and swapped it out in favor of riskier business. This extended kinship of cousins, aunts and uncles, brothers and sisters, parents, kids, and grandkids, has one thing in common—all members love to gamble. It started with scratch cards one holiday when everyone was broke. They each brought five scratch cards to their annual Christmas dinner at their favorite casino's buffet, and scratched them during dessert. Their collective win was $100, which they then blew on more scratch tickets.

This ritual is repeated every year—the only difference is how much they win and lose, and the way in which they lose it. They've bet on the horses and football, boxing, and dog racing. They've played blackjack and roulette, the slots and keno, Texas hold 'em, and local elections. Their biggest Christmas cash-in so far: $5,000, which they won playing video poker. Whatever they win, they split equally among the group. Their slogan: Next year, Megabucks!

THANKS-FOR-NOTHING GIVING

The worst thing you can get for Christmas is nothing. Nothing at all. In some ways it's even worse than spending Christmas alone, because you're not alone, you're with people too cheap or mean-spirited or just plain lazy to remember you at this special time of year. If the person who forgets you in this terrible way is your own mother, then this simply adds insult to injury.

Mary's mother from England has not given the California teacher a Christmas present since she was seven years old, when Mommie Dearest told her that Santa Claus was not real and now that she was a big girl, she wouldn't be getting any more gifts. Of course Mom always expects a Christmas gift from her daughter, because "only an ungrateful child would forget her mother." Mary never fails to give her mother a gift she knows the persnickety old woman will love—because, after all, she is her mother and getting her a present every year is proof that Mary has not turned out like dear old Mom.

IF YOU GET IT, YOU PAY FOR IT

There's nothing like receiving a wonderful, wonderfully expensive Christmas present from the one you love. Lovers know what your heart desires: a fantastic piece of jewelry, tickets to Rome (or wherever you'd most like to travel), even a new car. The ultimate luxury you'd never buy for yourself.

If you're lucky. Unfortunately, for some unlucky recipients, these so-called "perfect presents" come with an unbelievably high price tag. We know one woman whose ex-husband gave her a swell (read: pricey) hunter-green Jaguar for their fifth Christmas together. Unbeknownst to her, he'd put the car on her credit card—something she didn't find out until the bill showed up a month later *in her name*. When she confronted him about it, all he said was, "Merry Christmas." She loved the car, but it cost her $900 a month for the next five years.

Which is why he is now her ex-husband.

THE HIDDEN-AGENDA GIFT

Some people view gift giving as an opportunity to get what *they* really want. And what they really want is to change their partner in some way. Having failed the rest of the year to persuade their partner to make whatever change they've decided must be made, they use the holiday season to "incentivize" partners to give them what they really want. These gifts are often elaborate and expensive—but that doesn't hide the hidden agenda as completely as these gift givers often seem to think it does. The recipients almost always see the ruse beneath the wrapping—and resent their partners for it. Here are just a few of the "hidden agenda" stories we've heard.

The "You're Too Fat" Gift

These gifts are often presented in wrapping so fine it's hard to confirm the real intent. Who can complain about a week at a Canyon Ranch? A lifetime membership to Gold's Gym? A year's worth of tennis lessons at an exclusive tennis club? Confront your partner over gifts like these, and they'll accuse you of being ungrateful, of being hypersensitive, of looking a gift horse in the mouth. They only care about your health, your well-being, your quality of life.

Whatever. We know a woman from Sonoma, California, whose husband was so obsessed with her weight after giving birth to three kids in five years—*his* three kids, naturally—that he used every national holiday as an excuse to badger her about it. He bought her a Stairmaster, a week at a fat farm, even a $10,000 new wardrobe if she lost forty pounds. The subliminal—and not so subliminal—messages of these so-called gifts were not lost on our friend. She used the Stairmaster as a clothes rack; she snuck Twinkies into the fat farm; she rejected the new wardrobe in favor of her plus-size sweatpants. The happy ending: After their divorce several years later, she lost twenty pounds out of sheer happiness at her new freedom. She's kept it off, and is now happily married to a man who appreciates her curves. She's not skinny, but she looks and feels great. A happy footnote: Her ex is miserable with his new wife, a size-2 redhead who spends his money faster than he can make it.

The "You're Not Sophisticated Enough" Gift

Remember the story of Pygmalion, the sculptor who carved the perfect woman out of ivory, only to fall in love with her? Hint: This ancient Greek myth was retold by George Bernard Shaw in the famous play of the same name and the stunning Lerner and

Loewe musical version *My Fair Lady*, starring the incomparable Audrey Hepburn and Rex Harrison in the film version. Who could forget Hepburn's amazing transformation from poor, uneducated Cockney flower seller to elegant English lady of the house at the hands of the exacting Professor Higgins? Well, some partners not only remember it, they want to pull a little Professor Higgins themselves. They want to sculpt their own perfect lover out of their current mate—consequences be damned.

At first, these efforts may be welcomed by the partner, who can be flattered by all that attention. But sooner or later, the partner figures out that at the bottom of the makeover process is the unsettling realization that their own personal Professor Higgins believes that they're just not good enough the way they are. That they are not, in fact, loved for who they really are.

We know one such couple; we'll call them Harry and Helen. Harry is a sophisticated Manhattanite, an accountant with artistic aspirations whose idea of a good time is an avant-garde film followed by dinner at a five-star restaurant. On weekends you'll find him browsing art galleries and antiques shops, shopping on Fifth Avenue, and cooking up haute cuisine for friends for Sunday brunch. When he was called to Reno, Nevada, for a six-month job stint, he fell for Helen, a beautiful bartender at Caesar's Palace. The physical attraction—opposites do attract, you know!—was overwhelming. He married her, and took her home to New York, where he proceeded to "gentrify" his cute cowgirl. It all started innocently enough, with a Christmas gift certificate to Elizabeth Arden. He had Helen made over totally: new hair, new makeup, new clothes. And it didn't stop there: He signed her up for adult ed classes at the 92nd Street YMCA, provided elocution lessons to eliminate her twang, even enrolled her in charm school.

Within a couple of years, you wouldn't have recognized Helen: She dressed and moved beautifully, she spoke beautifully, she even debated the political issues of the day beautifully. Give her thirty minutes and the girl whose previous skills were limited to making a great blended margarita could throw an elegant dinner party together, do the *New York Times* crossword puzzle, and/or plan a successful fundraiser. Not to mention play a mean game of tennis. But an odd thing happened on the way to Helen's transformation: She fell out of love with Harry. In truth, he bored her. Last we heard, Helen had left him and was living in Rome with a medieval scholar—and Harry was seeing a beautician from the Bronx.

The Hidden Language of "You" Gifts

Spa trip = You're fat

Gym membership = You're out of shape

Yoga retreat = You're stressed out

Treadmill = Get your butt off the couch

Tuition = You're ignorant

Career-counselor session = Get a real job

Cosmetic surgery consult = You're ugly

Life-coach consult = Your life is a mess

Feng shui house call = Your house is a mess

Makeover = You are a mess

The Hidden Language of "I" Gifts

Sexy lingerie = I want to plan our honeymoon

Weekend getaway = I want to plan our affair

Therapy = I want you to be different

Prescription for Prozac = I want you to be happy

Driving lessons = I want you to be more independent

Babysitter = I want some alone time with you

Nanny = I want lots of alone time with you

Cooking lessons = I want dinner on the table

Chef = I want dinner on the table now

Marriage counseling = I want a divorce

The "You're Too Fat/Bald/Insert Imperfect Body Part Here" Gift

If you think that giving someone a cosmetic surgery gift certificate for Christmas is insensitive at the very least and wildly offensive at the very most, think again. Some 25 percent of people are thinking about giving their partner such a gift, according to Evolence, a "facial aesthetics specialty" company. Anecdotally, we know lots of people who've received cosmetic procedures as presents—some more happily than others. In Las Vegas, for example, teenage girls routinely beg their parents to fill their Christmas stockings with nose jobs and breast jobs. But in other relationships, particularly marital relationships, such gifts are not received so graciously.

A beautiful brunette we'll call Joanne from Palm Springs had the trim body of the tennis pro she was—but that wasn't good enough for her breast-obsessed husband. He managed to hide his obsession while they were dating, but from the minute the honeymoon ended he was on her to have a breast job. Granted, she was quite flat-chested, but it didn't bother her. She was proud of her fit body—and well aware of the appreciative glances she received at the tennis courts from admiring men. So she ignored her husband's snide remarks about her perky petite breasts. But when his best friend got his wife a breast job for Christmas, she knew she'd find the same offering under the tree. When she did, she knew that she could no longer sleep with a man who didn't love her body as much as she did. She left him, and found love with a leg man who lives for her tennis-toned gams.

We know one formerly hirsute guy from New York who lost his hair early on in his marriage. His wife hated his increasingly bald pate, and spent several holiday seasons trying to get him to do something about it. The first Christmas it was a hair weave, the second Christmas it was a very expensive toupee, the third Christmas it was hair transplants. Gary—we'll call him Gary—tried the hair weave and toupee, but drew the line at hair transplants. In a fit of pique, he shaved his head. His wife left him for a leonine banker—and Gary eventually found happiness with his divorce lawyer, who loves his "sexy sleek head."

Top Five Cosmetic Procedures for Women

Breast job

Nose job

Liposuction

Eyelid Surgery

Tummy Tuck

Top Five Cosmetic Procedures for Men

Nose job

Eyelid surgery

Liposuction

Hair transplantation

Male breast reduction

The "You've Got to Quit" Gift

Imagine you're going to your family holiday get-together, but when you get there you find yourself in the middle of an intervention—yours! This is a sneaky method, but if you're a substance abuser, odds are you know all about sneaky. Warren from Chicago, an alcoholic, faced this very situation one Christmas. He was angry, but he was also mortified. He agreed to check himself into rehab—and by the following Christmas he was clean and sober for the first time in a decade. So if this happens to you, bite the bullet and let your family help you. Because that's really what Christmas is all about.

The "Thank You for Not Smoking" Gift

If you get a nicotine patch for Christmas, you smoke too much. You know that smoking is bad for you, but you may not care. Unfortunately for you, there are two kinds of people in the world: smokers and nonsmokers. And the nonsmokers are now in charge, apparently for good. Our friend Larry started smoking in junior high school in Ohio, but gave it up when he moved to California—the Motherland of Nonsmokers—fifteen years later. There in Santa Cruz he met and married Honey, the girl of his dreams. Honey was a vegetarian yoga instructor who would no more smoke a cigarette than she'd eat a Big Mac or wear a mink coat. They were very happy together, until Larry lost his job and couldn't find another. Stressed out, he started sneaking a smoke whenever he walked the dog at night—and soon was up to two packs a day. By this time there was no hiding his habit from Honey. She was sympathetic at first, but soon had had enough. She got him a nicotine patch for Christmas, along with six sessions with a hypnotist. With her help, Larry quit smoking for good. He'll never know how or why he really quit—hypnotic suggestion, the patch, his love for Helen?—but he's glad he did.

THE DEAR JOHN CHRISTMAS CARD

Breaking up is hard to do, but getting dumped on Christmas Eve is hard to even imagine, much less suffer through. Several people we know have been unceremoniously abandoned just as the most festive time of year begins—sometimes in surprisingly creative, if cruel, ways. One sweet man from Baltimore we know received a FedEx package Christmas Eve, just hours before he planned to propose to his girlfriend. In the package was a Christmas card with a short note that read, *"I'm sorry but I've met someone else. Sarah."* He tried to call her, but she wouldn't return his calls. He spent his Christmas alone—and he never saw Sarah again. Eventually he met someone else, and got married. But even now, all these years later, he opens each Christmas card he receives with a vague sense of dread.

THE ART OF REGIFTING

In today's return to a "waste not, want not" thrift, regifting has become an economic necessity—even perhaps your patriotic duty. But before you do any real regifting, you need to learn the rules. There's much more to it than simply passing off something you hate to the next unsuspecting victim. Lorna of Chicago is the queen of regifting. She swears that if you do it right, your friends and family will never know that they've been regifted. Here are her foolproof guidelines:

Always repackage the items. If you're passing along a bottle of wine, put it in a pretty cloth wine bag. Place candles in pretty holders; wrap clothes in lavender-scented paper before wrapping them; present jewelry in a silver, glass, or wooden box lined in velvet. And gift cards fit nicely into Christmas tins.

Top Ten Regifted Christmas Presents

Clothing   Cookbooks

Housewares   Candles

Gift baskets   Fruitcake

Picture frames   Gift cards

Jewelry   Booze

Source: www.regiftable.com

Personalize items whenever you can. Insert a photo of yourself in a regifted picture frame; fill a regifted vase with the recipient's favorite flowers; embroider monograms on linens and clothing. Write your own poem to tuck into a book of poetry; print out a favorite family recipe to slip into a cookbook; add a homemade bookmark to a novel.

Group like items together in impromptu gift baskets. What might seem like a cheap gift on its own can take on a whole new gold standard of regifting when you augment it. Pair scented soaps with body lotion and guest towels, a sleep mask with pajamas, ceramic mugs with gourmet coffee. Any loose gifts—toiletries, housewares, gourmet food items—can be grouped together in gift baskets. Get creative: Fill a cookie jar with homemade cookies, a toolbox with screwdrivers, a watering can with seed packets and bulbs.

Don't forget the fixer-uppers. Don't just regift unwanted gifts you've recently received from others. Go through your closets, your drawers, your garage, and your attic. Most of us have lots of stuff we've long forgotten about that other people would love. Polish up the jewelry you never wear, and never really liked, and give it to someone it would better suit. Reframe that old concert poster your nephew would love; dry-clean that 1970s polyester print dress for your colleague who loves vintage clothing; repaint that peeling rocking chair for a pregnant friend's nursery.

THE "I'M TOO BROKE FOR CHRISTMAS" GIFT

When you're really too broke for Christmas, but you can't not remember your friends and family at this special time of year, take regifting up a notch. This means giving away some of your favorite things in the name of Christmas love. That's what single mom Elizabeth from Massachusetts did one year when she was simply too strapped to buy presents for her three children. To her eldest daughter, she gave her most beloved—and expensive!—jewelry, a lovely string of real pearls that she'd worn at her wedding. Her son, an aspiring writer, got Elizabeth's first edition of Hemingway's *A Moveable Feast*. And to her youngest daughter Elizabeth gave her childhood sterling silver charm bracelet, with the charms she'd collected on her travels throughout Europe with her parents. In passing along some of her highly prized possessions—in terms of both financial and sentimental value—Elizabeth turned the Christmas That Almost Wasn't into the Heirloom Christmas her kids will never forget.

THE CHARLIE BROWN CHRISTMAS TREE

Every year we spend some $2.5 billion on Christmas trees. That's more than 31 million real trees, and 17.4 million fake trees. But for the Ritter family from Indiana, all the money in the world can't buy what they call a Charlie Brown Christmas tree. Fifteen years ago, Bob and Jayne Ritter were a young couple with a new baby. They couldn't afford a Christmas tree, and were prepared to go without one. But on the way home from work on Christmas Eve, Bob decided to splurge and get one anyway. The new baby would like the ornaments and lights, he thought. So he went to the tree lot—but it was closed and empty. Then he spotted an abandoned tree near a dumpster at the back of the lot. It was a scrawny little thing, not much to look at. But it was a tree—and apparently it was free. Bob took it home to their little apartment, and Jayne nearly smothered the little tree in blinking lights and ornaments and garlands and tinsel. The baby was spellbound by the little Charlie Brown Christmas tree—and thus began a Ritter tradition. Every year, the Ritters wait until Christmas Eve to get their tree—and every year they find the runt of the litter to bring home. They shower it with love and decorations, and tell the story of their very first Charlie Brown Christmas tree. It's a Ritter ritual now, one that their whole family enjoys.

Most Popular Christmas Trees

Fake tree: They come in all shapes and sizes and colors, some complete with lights and ornaments. They don't drop needles, and they last a lifetime. Longer, even, which is why they're not as eco-friendly as you might think.

Balsam fir: With its dark-green long-lasting needles, this attractively shaped tree boasts a lovely fragrance.

Fraser fir: This beautiful blue-green tree from the East boasts all of the characteristics of its closely related cousin the balsam fir, with the added advantage of its unique coloring.

Douglas fir: This Western tree—which is not related to the true firs—is one of the most popular Christmas trees in the United States. These trees can live for a thousand years, thanks to their thick bark.

Noble fir: This beautifully symmetrical tree from the North-west is very popular. Its lovely greenery is popular not only for Christmas trees, but also for garlands, wreaths, and swags.

Eastern white pine: The state tree of both Maine and Michigan, the largest pine in America has little scent compared to its counterparts, so it's said to be a good choice for those subject to allergies.

Scotch pine: This hardy, long-lasting tree is the most common Christmas tree in the United States. Its strong branches make it ideal for heavy ornaments.

Colorado blue spruce: The state tree of Colorado and Utah, this lovely blue tree is one of the most popular to be sold as a living tree for replanting in one's yard after the holiday.

Eastern red cedar: This tree is really a juniper; it grows in the Great Plains and Western states such as Nebraska, Oklahoma, Texas, and Kansas. It's usually only available for sale at choose-and-cut tree farms.

Virginia pine: This common Southern pine is a favorite nesting spot for woodpeckers. Its dense foliage makes it one of the most popular Christmas trees in the South.

Source: National Christmas Tree Association

THE CAMPBELL CHRISTMAS BAKE-OFF

Christmas is the one time of year most of us refuse to count calories. We indulge ourselves, gorging on turkey and ham and prime rib, stuffing and mashed potatoes topped with gravy, eggnog and punch, shrimp cocktail and chips and dip and cheese and crackers. And let's not forget dessert—oh, the desserts! We pack on the pounds—an average of seven to ten pounds each!—every Christmas season downing all those fattening entrees, appetizers, and desserts. At the Campbell house in Ohio, however, they've discovered a way to have their cake—without eating too much of it.

Every year they hold the Campbell Christmas Bake-Off. This is an elaborate affair, in which all the Campbells participate: parents, kids, grandkids, cousins, aunts, uncles, even the great-grandparents. A family known for its love of baked goods, the Campbells were all obviously born with the sweet tooth gene. They've been avid bakers all for generations; the family recipes for red velvet cake, pecan pie, and chocolate mousse are closely guarded secrets.

The ritual begins in early December, when each of the Campbells begins to perfect their new Yuletide recipes. Every possible kind of dessert is represented: pies and tarts, cakes and petit fours, puddings and mousses, cookies and brownies, candy and taffy, donuts and sweet rolls—you name it, the Campbells can make it. By the last Sunday of Advent, the Campbells are ready to bake their way to culinary confection. That's when they gather at Grandmama Campbell's Victorian house and eat themselves into a sugar coma as they taste every dessert. Grandmama, the Diva of Desserts, proclaims the winner, whose victorious recipe is added to the Campbell Classic Cookbook. All the leftover dessert—if there's any left, that is—goes to the local shelter.

"MERRY CHRISTMAS, YOU'RE FIRED!"

Lots of people get laid off every year around the holidays, given its unfortunate coinciding with the fourth quarter. But for Sharon and her husband, David, of Australia, getting laid off from their jobs at the train station the week of Christmas came as a shock. It was especially surprising for Sharon, as she'd saved the boss's life just a few months before. Sharon is a registered nurse. When her boss suffered a severe heart attack right there at the station, Sharon medicated him, gave him oxygen, and contacted the closest emergency services in the next town. While they waited for the ambulance, her boss's condition worsened, so Sharon and David carried the man to their car, and raced toward the hospital. They met the ambulance halfway, and her boss survived, thanks to Sharon's ministrations. Yet fewer than ninety days later, she and her husband were let go. They were given two weeks to move themselves and their five kids out of the company house. And you thought your boss was a Scrooge.

The December Pink Slip

In 2008 533,000 Americans lost their jobs in December.

"MERRY CHRISTMAS, YOU'RE DIVORCED!"

Never get married on Christmas—or any holiday, for that matter. If you do, and it doesn't work out, you're setting yourself up for a lifetime of bad memories. Remember, nearly half of all marriages end in divorce—so this really could happen to you. It happened to a friend of ours, a sweetheart of a guy named Kevin from Phoenix. Kevin's fiancée was determined to get married on Christmas Eve at midnight, and she talked Kevin—who normally would have known better, as he'd already been divorced once—into it. It was a lovely wedding, a small affair at the California bungalow they shared together. The fiancée turned out to be an odd girl, a serious-minded, unhappy young woman who was looking for a daddy, not a husband. Five Christmases later she ran off to Florida with her boss, a man old enough to be her father. She'd gotten the daddy she'd wanted—and Kevin got a Christmas full of pain. He's spent Christmas alone ever since. So whatever you do, pick a no-name day to get married. That way, if you end up single again, you'll just hate November 18, or March 19, or August 3. Not December 25.

Chapter Five
JOLLY OLD ST. NICK . . .
AND FRIENDS

Wild and Wacky Variations on the Santa Claus Theme

Whether he's a chubby, pink-cheeked darling with long white hair and a beard or a slim, white-robed grandfatherly presence, dear old Santa Claus is a favorite Christmas tradition. Although similar Santa Claus figures have arisen from myths around the world, the Americanized Santa Claus evolved from a combination of traditions—primarily *Sinterklaas,* from the Dutch Netherlanders who settled in New York. Ours is pretty tame, especially compared to some European traditions that include St. Nick's evil twin—the devil! Let's begin with good old St. Nick, and work our way up to the devil.

> *I never believed in Santa Claus because I knew no white dude would come into my neighborhood after dark.*
>
> —COMEDIAN DICK GREGORY

THE LEGEND OF ST. NICHOLAS

Many European holidays begin with the celebrated return of St. Nicholas, the sacred protector of children who was so, well, saintly, God rewarded him by allowing him to return once a year to bestow gifts on all the good little boys and girls. From the Netherlands to Albania, St. Nicholas comes on December 6, his feast day (oddly enough, a feast day is not celebrated on the day a saint was born, but on the day the saint died and returned to heaven), a special holiday apart from Christmas. Typically, he arrives on St. Nicholas's Eve, December 5, leaving small gifts and edible goodies. St. Nicholas (or *Nicolo* or *Niklaus*) is dressed similarly to a Catholic bishop, with flowing robes and a pointy hat called a miter. He typically travels with angels or cherubs, and often with his evil twin in the form of a devilish character that punishes, or at least threatens to punish, naughty children. During the year, those sweet little angels at St. Nicholas's side record each child's good and bad deeds in a large book. In some areas, children still have to answer religious questions before being rewarded with gifts or goodies.

How to Spot St. Nicholas

He's wearing a miter, a tall pointed hat typically worn by bishops.

He's carrying a crosier, a hooked shepherd's staff, also carried by bishops (and the shape of candy canes), to signify his desire to shepherd children to safety.

He's carrying around three gold balls, or gold coins or moneybags, to provide dowries for impoverished maidens. Sometimes oranges or apples are used to represent the gold.

Three maidens follow him around hoping they'll receive the dowry money.

Children often accompany him—because he's their patron saint.

Sailors or anchors or ships are nearby—because he's also their patron saint.

He's carrying a large book, the Book of the Gospels or the Holy Scriptures—or a book in which he records children's behavior.

He has a shoe fetish. Children will place their shoes filled with carrots, turnips, or hay on windowsills so St. Nicholas can feed his horse or donkey. St. Nicholas replaces the donkey food with candied treats.

HOW SANTA CLAUS ONCE MADE HIS ENTRANCE

In the 1600s, those prurient Puritans declared it a crime to mention St. Nicholas's name. They also forbade anyone to exchange gifts, light candles, or sing Christmas carols. Luckily, Dutch immigrants in New York eventually introduced the legend of *Sinterklaas* to more open-minded Americans. In 1804, the newly founded New York Historical Society chose St. Nicholas as their patron saint, and some of its members adopted the Dutch practice of gift giving at Christmas. Five years later, eminent author Washington Irving, under the pseudonym Diedrich Knickerbocker, wrote *A History of New York*, in which he portrayed St. Nicholas galloping into the bustling metropolis on a horse. Three years later, for whatever reason, Irving decided to revise the story to have good old St. Nicholas float over the trees in a wagon. In 1821, William Gilley printed a poem about Santeclaus, a kindly figure dressed in fur who drove a sleigh drawn by a single reindeer.

Saddle Up

In the Netherlands, Sinterklaas arrives on a large white horse, a schimmel, which he rides around the countryside to visit schools and homes. Sometimes a white horse is also with St. Nicholas in Belgium, Germany, and Poland. In France, Belgium, Luxembourg, and Switzerland, St. Nicholas leads a donkey laden with baskets full of treats and toys for children.

Papa, Can You Hear Me?

Christian children in China hang up muslin stockings that are specially made so Dun Che Lao Ren, or "Christmas Old Man," can fill them with wonderful gifts. Santa Claus may also be called Lan Khoong-Khoong (Nice Old Father).

A SANTA BY ANY NAME . . .

Around the world Santa Claus has many monikers. Here are a few to ponder:

- England—Kris Kringle or Father Christmas
- France—Père Noel (Father Christmas)
- Italy—Babbo Natale (Father Christmas)
- Germany—Weihnachtsmann or Sankt Nikolaus
- Sweden—Jultomten (Christmas Brownie)
- Belgium—Sinterklaas, who visits children on December 6; and De Kerstman (Christmas Man), who visits on December 26
- Chile—Viejo Pascuerro
- Japan—Santa Kurohsu; Hoteiosho is a Buddhist priest who bears gifts
- Hawaii—Kanakaloka

CAN WE HAVE A SCORECARD?

Some regions have such complicated Christmas characters that it's hard to remember who's who. For example, in Russia, Ded Moroz (aka Grandfather Frost), accompanied by his grand-daughter Snegurochka (aka Miss Snow or Snow Maiden), visits Russian children. Although many oral stories abound about the Russian Babushka, or elderly woman, no such figure appears in any Russian Christmas literature.

In Germany, children leave letters on their windowsills for Christkind, an angelic winged figure dressed in white robes and wearing a golden crown, who they believe was sent by the Christ child to bring them gifts. Weihnachtsmann (Christmas Man), who looks very much like Santa Claus, comes bearing gifts on Christmas Eve. German Americans sometimes have Belsnickle, who brings presents for the children, but also taps "bad children" with his switch if they have misbehaved.

SANTA, SANTA WHEREFORE ART THOU?

In 1955, a Sears store in Colorado Springs inadvertently ran the phone number of the Continental Air Defense (CONAD) in a newspaper advertisement encouraging children to call a

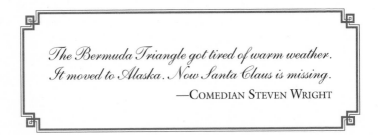

The Bermuda Triangle got tired of warm weather. It moved to Alaska. Now Santa Claus is missing.

—COMEDIAN STEVEN WRIGHT

Santa Claus hotline. Luckily, when the first calls came in a kind-hearted colonel instructed his staff to give any children who called Santa's current position in the night sky. When CONAD merged with Canada and became the North American Aerospace Defense Command (NORAD), they continued the tradition, which goes on to this day. About 800 volunteers staff the phone lines (and now the web). In 2006, they fielded over half a million calls and over 12,500 e-mails from 210 territories.

If your children (or you) need further proof that Santa is on his way, here's a summary of what NORAD posts on their Web site:

Santa is tracked using a powerful radar system with forty-seven installations strung across the northern border of North America that pick up Santa as he leaves the North Pole on Christmas Eve. Once Santa has lifted off, satellites located in a geo-synchronous orbit at 22,300 miles above the Earth track Santa using infrared sensors that pick up the heat of Rudolph's nose. Then, ultra-cool high-tech high-speed digital cameras they call Santa Cams are pre-positioned at many places around the world. NORAD only uses these cameras one night a year—Christmas Eve—to capture images of Santa and the reindeer as they make their journey around the world. They immediately download the images to their Web site for people around the world to see. When Santa crosses into North America, NORAD jet fighters take off out of Newfoundland to intercept, welcome, and escort Santa and his famous reindeer, Dasher, Dancer, Prancer, Vixen, Comet, Cupid, Donner, Blitzen, and Rudolph.

The NORAD Web site (www.noradsanta.org) now gets well over one billion hits per year.

POOR OLD SANTA CLAUS

According to the Amalgamated Order of Real Bearded Santas (AORBS), Father Christmas has to put up with a lot of abuse during the festive season. After polling over 330 of their members, here are a few of their findings:

- Number of Santas peed on by children: 34 percent
- Number of Santas who have been sneezed or coughed on up to ten times each day: 60 percent
- Number of Santas who have had up to ten children cry while on their lap each day: 74 percent
- Number of Santas who had their facial hair tugged by children each day: 90 percent

The findings were so shocking that pretzel purveyor Auntie Anne's distributed Santa survival kits to shopping centers across America, including essential items ranging from hand sanitizers to an official reindeer pooper-scooper.

THE GREAT WARRIOR COMES BEARING GIFTS

Move over, Santa Claus. In the Miller household of Nevada, the Great Warrior appears every Thanksgiving to reward good little warriors everywhere (or at least within shouting distance of the dinner table). The Great Warrior—aka retired paratrooper and devoted grandfather Miller—represents the noble and courageous spirit of the great fearless Apache leader Geronimo. Geronimo was as renowned for his amazing escapes as he was for his courage; he once made a fast getaway by jumping off Medicine Bluff on his Cadillac horse in Fort Sill, Oklahoma. This moment was immortalized in the film *Geronimo*—and

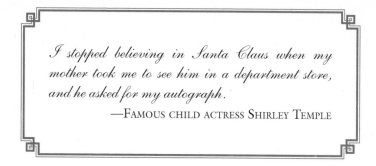
later viewed by the first paratrooper battalion in the U.S. Army. Moved by Geronimo's derring-do, Private Aubrey Eberhardt yelled "Geronimo!" as he made his first jump. Others followed suit, and Geronimo became the inspiration for paratroopers everywhere—including the good little warrior children, grand-children, and great-grandchildren of the Miller household, who receive gifts from the Great Warrior every year.

THE ANTI-SANTA

American children don't know how lucky they have it. If they behave badly around Christmas, their sweet-cheeked Santa still slides down the chimney, though he might gobble up their cookies or stiff the gift-expecting kiddies. Believe us, kids, it could be worse—a lot worse.

In parts of Austria, Bavaria, and Switzerland, badly behaved children face the wrath of a seven-foot-tall hairy, horned devilish creature called Krampus—the ultimate diabolical anti-Santa, who roams the streets dragging chains and waggling sticks, threaten-ing to spank naughty children or shove them into sacks and whisk them away. With his goat's head, cloven feet, and grotesquely long red tongue, Krampus may have been spawned from a Greek satyr, and—trust us, spoiled Americans—he's no cheerful fellow.

On December 5, the eve of St. Nicholas's Day when good little children will awaken to find gifts in their shoes, adults celebrate Krampuslauf by dressing as Krampus—wearing goat- or sheepskin getups, carved masks, and horns—and roaming the streets, waving cowbells, flailing their sticks, and menacing passersby. In some towns, kids endure a gauntlet, dodging swats from tree branches as they dash past a line of Krampus wannabes. It's all in good fun, they say, but many revelers also choose that night to drink heavily, which has led to taunting the angry Krampus and many mock beatings. Today, the faux-Krampus crowd is more likely downing pints of beer than rattling cowbells to frighten children, unless you count the town of Schladminger, where more than a thousand goat-men roam the streets, playfully teasing (flirting with) the town's young women.

Krampus is derived from an old German word, *Krampen*, meaning claw. During the Inquisition, impersonating a devil was punishable by death, so Krampus went underground. Luckily, the tradition continued in remote mountain areas and resurfaced in the seventeenth century, when Krampus was permitted, once again, to serve as St. Nicholas's evil alter ego.

Krampus by Any Other Name

In Southern Germany, Krampus is dubbed Pelzebock or Pelznickel; in the northwest he's Hans Muff; in Rhineland he's Bartel or the Wild Bear; in Silesia he's Gumphinkel.

Bring On the Angels

In Belgium, Germany, Poland, Czech Republic, Slovakia, Ukraine, and Austria, angels often accompany St. Nicholas. In Czech and Slovak tradition the angel is there to keep St. Nick's other companion, that nasty devil, under control so he can't harm the good little children.

JUST WAIT TILL RUPRECHT GETS HOME

In other regions of Germany, Ruprecht or *Knecht Ruprecht* represents the dark side of good old St. Nick. He's essentially St. Nicholas's servant and helper. He may carry the sack, but he also carries and wags the proverbial rod, threatening to smack naughty children. Since he slides down the chimney, his face is conveniently dark and sooty—all the better to scare those bad little girls and boys. As the holidays crank up, harried parents will parry about his name, proclaiming, "Just wait until Ruprecht comes."

SANTA TRAUMA

Long before waterboarding or PTSD, a clever president tortured his adversaries by employing, you guessed it, dear old Santa Claus. In the 1860s, *Harper's Weekly* illustrator Thomas Nast created images of Santa for the magazine's Christmas editions that quickly became iconic—and ran annually for thirty years. During the civil war, president Abraham Lincoln asked

Nast to create a drawing of Santa hanging out with Union soldiers. This image of Santa supporting the enemy had such a demoralizing influence on the Confederate army that some accused Lincoln of committing what would be called psychological warfare today.

SINISTER SANTA

In 1845, a Netherlander wrote a book called *Sinterklaas en Zijn Knecht,* about a character named Zwarte Piet (Black Peter). Zwarte Piet basically served as Sinterklaas's enforcer, a scary figure who would bundle up naughty girls and boys and take them back to Spain, where Sinterklaas lived in the off-season. In some areas, Sinterklaas arrives on the eve of St. Nicholas's Day in a steamship, his trusty, eh, helper (some say slave) by his side. Originating during the Netherlands's colonial days, the racist aspects of the custom have been downplayed in recent decades, and it's become more fashionable to describe Black Peter as a black-faced chimney sweep covered in soot. But charges of racism still follow Black Peter, as he is often portrayed with an Afro and exaggerated features.

THE BUTCHER OF PARIS

In France and Luxembourg, an evil character known as *Père Fouettard* accompanies St. Nicholas. *Père Fouettard* stems from the myth of an evil butcher who lured three innocent children lost in the woods into his shop, where he chopped them up and stored them in salted brine. When St. Nicholas arrived and touched the fingertips of the children, he was able to restore and rescue the children. As punishment, the evil butcher was

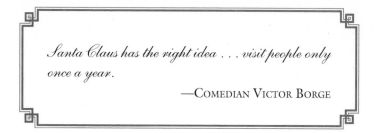

Santa Claus has the right idea . . . visit people only once a year.

—Comedian Victor Borge

forever condemned to trot along after St. Nicholas—in chains, so he couldn't hurt any more children. Like all French words, his name holds many meanings, connecting him to Mr. Bogeyman, spanking, and switches.

WHAT A SCHMUTZ

Who'da thunk peaceful Switzerland would also harbor a Christmas devil? Known as Schmutzli, this fellow isn't near as scary as Krampus or Black Peter, but he wears all brown—a brown robe, brown hair, and beard—and a face darkened by coating it with lard and smearing it with soot. This crusty old guy carries a switch and a sack to threaten naughty children. Really bad children are smuggled away in the sack to the woods, where Schmutzli gobbles them up. Today everything is more *PC*, with a kinder, gentler Schmutzli who no longer beats or kidnaps children. Like other bad Santas, he just shakes a stick at them.

A DAY IN THE PARK WITH GEORGE

In the days of ancient Rome, the festival of Saturnalia often included a parade of masters and slaves, in which the masters dressed in fantastical costumes and the slaves dressed like their masters. Together, they'd parade through the streets, going from neighbor to neighbor to celebrate the reap of the harvest. As Christian celebrations gained favor, the once-raucous Saturnalia festival was banished to December 26 so as not to tarnish celebrations of the birth of Christ. Swedish immigrants known as Mummers brought the tradition to Philadelphia, where they instituted the Mummers Parade and stretched the celebration to the entire week between Christmas and New Year's. During his first term as president (served in Philadelphia), George Washington partook of the Mummers' celebration, which meant a whole lot of people dressed like George wandered drunkenly through the streets, meeting and greeting fellow celebrants. By the Civil War, when owning slaves was no longer fashionable, the celebration had lost favor, but today feisty Mummers still take to the streets for their annual Mummers Parade and spend at least one day hoisting drinks in all manner of bars—from comic clubs to nightclubs and fancy restaurants.

SO WHAT'S WITH RUDOLPH?

In 1939, a Montgomery Ward copywriter named Robert L. May who had been taunted as a child for being shy and slight created the tale of Rudolph, an ostracized, um, *underdog* reindeer whose shiny red nose catapulted him to stardom. It seems Santa's other eight reindeer couldn't find their way on a foggy Christmas Eve until they happened upon Rudolph, whose red nose lit the way. The poem was first released as a giveaway for Montgomery Ward customers. In 1949 songwriter Johnny Marks penned "Rudolph, the Red-Nosed Reindeer," relocating Rudolph to the North Pole, where he was banned from those charming reindeer games. The song became a huge hit for cowboy crooner Gene Autry, and, second only to the astronomically popular "White Christmas," remains one of the most popular Christmas songs of all time.

WHERE OH WHERE DOTH SANTA GO?

Each culture has its version of a mythological Santa Claus, and each Santa retreats to a land far, far away. For Netherlanders, that faraway land was sunny Spain—lucky Santa! For Americans, a Thomas Nast *Harper's Weekly* illustration depicting a young girl dropping a letter addressed to "Santa Claus, North Pole," wed our jolly old man to the rigors of a frozen tundra, and a toy factory suspiciously staffed by miniature elves, somewhere deep beneath the never-ending ice and snow. Neither of these would suit the French-speaking region of Bulle, Switzerland, however. Oh, no. Once their St. Nicholas has delivered his gifts, he—and his accompanying cherubs—float, ever so gracefully, back to heaven!

SANTA SCHMANTA,
WHERE'S LA BEFANA?

Italy's beloved La Befana, aka the Christmas witch, wanted nothing to do with the North Pole. She lives in Urbania, where locals host an annual festival in her honor that attracts 30,000 to 50,000 people, depending on the weather, from January 2 to 6. Over 100 of the, shall we say, homeliest women swing from the towers of the main square, juggle and dance, or simply stroll through the streets with their brooms, greeting festival-goers. Urbania notes that it doesn't have 100 ugly women and proudly reveals that their prettiest girls vie for the honor. To prepare, they don oversized dirty, patched ankle-length dresses (that they stuff with cotton), tie babushka-style scarves around their heads, and rub soot on their faces. It's such a coveted role that men have been known to slip amongst the ranks.

IS SANTA IN LAPLAND?

Realizing that reindeer can't graze at the North Pole, Finnish radio host Markus Rautio decided in 1927 that Santa Claus actually lives on Lapland's Korvatunturi, also known as the Ear Fell because it resembles, well, bunny ears. The better to hear the children with, Rautio decided. Since the 1950s, the Finnish have claimed that Santa hangs out at Napapiiri, near Rovaniemi. By 1985, Santa was "spotted" so often in Napapiiri that he opened a sort of Santa Claus branch office there. Supposedly, he shows up every day to field the requests of good little boys and girls from throughout the world. Santa's "Main Post Office" receives children's letters from the four corners of the world.

Santa's out in the Cold

Hit by the global recession and facing a sharp economic downturn in 2009, the country of Finland announced that it was selling its 32 percent stake in Santapark in Lapland, home to Father Christmas, to local investors.

Chapter Six

EAT, DRINK, AND BE MERRY

How to Grog, Nog, and Glogg Your Way through the Holidays

Throughout the centuries, in countries around the world, food has been an integral part of the celebration. Whether it's roasted goose or whale blubber, food eaten at holiday time carries weight in our culture and in our memories. Much of the food we eat during the holidays comes from old wives' tales and traditions handed down for hundreds of years—and then there's always Aunt Minnie's moldy pudding or Aunt Bonnie's black buns, Maman's elegant escargot or Grandma Gertie's lutefisk.

AROUND THE WORLD WITH ALKA-SELTZER

In the United States, a typical Christmas feast can contain a variety of foods, including turkey, ham, chicken, or goose, but other countries have their own favorites. Here's a sampling—sans the plates, forks, napkins, and Alka-Seltzer:

England: Roasted turkey
Denmark: Roasted goose
Greece: Leg of lamb
Hungary: Chicken *paprikash*
Italy: Seven fishes, including a fish stew called *zuppa di pesce*

Ireland: Oyster stew

New Zealand: Picnic food eaten on the beach

Ghana: *Fufu* (rice and yam paste with okra stew and meat)

Greenland: Whale blubber

Sicily: Eel

Norway: Codfish

Poland: *Oplatek* (bread with a holy picture pressed into the surface)

Ukraine: *Kutya* (meatless porridge)

Venezuela: Bread filled with ham and raisins

Vietnam: Chicken soup

Let It Burn

The Jewish holiday Hanukkah is an eight-day Festival of Light that features fatty foods fried in oil to remind celebrants of the oil that burned in the temple for eight days.

SHAKESPEARE À LA MODE

Even though they were considered modest at the time, Shakespeare's Christmas feasts at Ingatestone certainly put turducken to shame. In *Dining with William Shakespeare*, Madge Lorwin notes that there were "Six boiled and three roast pieces of beef, a neck of mutton, a loin and breast of pork, a goose, four coneys [rabbits] and eight warden pies [pear pies colored with saffron]. For supper, five joints of mutton, a neck of pork, two coneys, a woodcock, and a venison pasty were served."

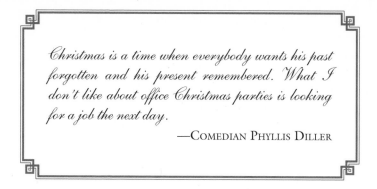

Christmas is a time when everybody wants his past forgotten and his present remembered. What I don't like about office Christmas parties is looking for a job the next day.

—COMEDIAN PHYLLIS DILLER

THE DEVIL WEARS SUGAR

In America, we bake butter-rich sugar cookies shaped like trees, bells, stars, Santa Claus, reindeer, and all things that signify a yummy, totally PC Christmas. In Austria, they also bake spiced cookies and mold chocolates into the shape of St. Nicholas, who brings presents on December 6, but they also bestow the same, um, honor on St. Nicholas's evil twin, Krampus. Krampus is one scary fellow, sporting horns and a long red tongue. Makes one wonder what those tasty specialties topped with colored icing, fruit, and nuts really look like. Even funnier, they also craft the likeness of St. Nicholas and Krampus out of prunes.

OH BRING US SOME FIGGY PUDDING

You've heard of aged fruitcake, but aged pudding? An ancient English tradition involves making a pudding one month before Christmas, and literally hanging it in some dark, cool corner of the house where it can age without being disturbed. The recipe varies but boils down to this: Mix together dried fruit, butter, sugar, eggs, breadcrumbs, brandy, and spices. Wrap the mixture in a flour-covered calico cloth and boil it for six hours. When it

Puddin' Sausage

Traditional Christmas puddings date back to the fifteenth century, but they were about as far as one could travel from the dainty puddings we buy in gourmet shops or boil on our stovetops. In those days, when they made pudding they made enough to feed an army. The cook hauled out the washtub—which we presume they washed and rinsed with boiled water before tossing in the ingredients. The very earliest puddings consisted of chopped-up meat, suet, oatmeal, and spices—worse yet, they were wrapped and boiled in the intestines of a sheep or pig, sort of a sausage pudding, if you will. Puddings as we know them began to appear in the sixteenth century and were more often wrapped in cloth bags.

cools, hang the pudding bundle in a dry place until Christmas. You want to tuck it away in a corner where no one will break the seal or touch it. Doing so can cause mold, in which case you'll have icky green Christmas pudding. Note: The bundle can be so heavy it requires two people to hoist it into the hanging space, and to take it down a month later. On Christmas, boil the pudding again for two hours and serve with cream or custard mixed with brandy—lots of brandy.

The Christmas Pudding Madness of King George

Purportedly, this recipe dates back to 1714, when it was concocted to celebrate King George's first Christmas.

- 1 pound eggs, beaten
- 1½ pounds shredded suet
- 1 pound dried plums
- 1 pound raisins
- 1 pound mixed peel, orange or lemon
- 1 pound currants
- 1 pound sultanas [golden raisins]
- 1 pound flour
- 1 pound sugar
- 1 pound breadcrumbs
- 1 teaspoon cinnamon
- ½ teaspoon grated nutmeg
- ½ pint milk
- ½ teaspoon of salt
- juice of 1 lemon
- a large glass of brandy

Mix all ingredients together and let stand for 12 hours. Boil for 8 hours, and boil again on Christmas Day for 2 hours. This will yield 9 pounds of pudding.

MYSTERY MEAT

In the *Oxford Companion to Food*, Alan Davidson writes, "The earliest mince pie was a small medieval pastry called a chewette, which contained chopped meat of liver, or fish on fast days, mixed with chopped hard-boiled egg and ginger that was baked or fried. To enrich and extend the filling, they added dried fruit

Old Fashioned Mince Pie
From *The Art of Cookery Made Plain and Easy*, Hannah Glasse, 1747

Mincemeat:

Three Pounds of Suet shredded very fine and chopped as small as possible

Two Pounds Raisins chopped as fine as possible

Two Pounds of Currants, nicely picked, washed, rubbed, and dried at the Fire,

Half a hundred of fine Pippins [apples], pared, cored, and chopped small,

Half a Pound of fine sugar pounded fine

¼ of an Ounce of Mace

¼ of an Ounce of Cloves

One pint of Brandy and half a pint of Sack [sherry]

Mix together in a stone-pot. It will keep good four months.

and other sweet ingredients. By the 16th century minced or shred pies, as they were then known, had become a Christmas specialty. The beef was sometimes partly or wholly replaced by suet from the mid-17th century onwards, and meat effectively disappeared from mincemeat on both sides of the Atlantic in the 19th century. In Colonial America these pies were made in the fall and sometimes frozen throughout winter."

Pie:

Take a little dish, something bigger than a soup-plate, lay a very thin crust all over it, lay a thin layer of mincemeat, and then a thin layer of citron [lemon] cut very thin, then another layer of mince-meat topped with a thin layer of orange-peel cut thin, and another layer of mincemeat. Squeeze half the juice of a fine Seville orange, or lemon, and pour in three spoonfuls of red wine; lay on your [top] crust, and bake it nicely.

These Pies eat finely cold. If you make them in little patties, mix your meat and sweet-meats accordingly: if you choose meat in your pies, parboil a Neat's tongue, peel it, and chop the meat as finely as possible, and mix with the rest; or two pounds of the inside of a surloin or beef boiled.

It's Plum Good

An English Christmas dinner resembles American menus, with turkey and stuffing, but instead of pecan or pumpkin pies, they favor mince pies and plum puddings. These pies contain raisins and currants that have been "plummed," or plumped up, by soaking them in warm brandy.

A PLUM ASSIGNMENT

Plum puddings can be traced back to the early 15th century. The first types were not specifically associated with Christmas. The original form, plum pottage, was made from chopped beef or mutton, onions, perhaps other root vegetables, and dried fruit. Surprisingly, it was served at the beginning of the meal. When new kinds of dried fruit became available in Britain, first raisins, then prunes in the 16th century, they were added. In the 16th century variants were made with white meat, and gradually the meat was replaced by suet. The root vegetables disappeared, although some still sneak one carrot into the pudding. It became linked with Christmas in the 1670s and was known as "Christmas pottage." The old plum pottage continued to be made into the 18th century, and both versions were still served as a first course rather than as a dessert—to fill up hungry bellies. The traditional Christmas pudding recipe has been more or less established since the 19th century.—*Oxford Companion to Food*, Alan Davidson

Christmas Plum Pudding Cure for Witches

The cook would make a little hole in the top and fill it with brandy, then light it, and serve it in a blaze. In olden time a sprig of arbutus, with a red berry on it, was stuck in the middle, and a twig of variegated holly, with berries, placed on each side—to keep away witches. If well made, Christmas plum pudding will be good for twelve months.

—CASSELL'S DICTIONARY OF COOKERY, 1875

Stir It Up

Christmas puddings were made in England on what they called "Stir-Up Sunday," the last Sunday before Advent, which is considered the final day on which one can make the Christmas fruitcakes and puddings that require time to age before being served. For luck, each member of the family took a turn stirring the pudding, using a special wooden spoon to honor Christ's crib. Stirrers would move the spoon in a clockwise motion, close their eyes, and make a wish.

Stirring Prayer

Stir up, we beseech thee, O Lord, the wills of thy faithful people, that they plenteously bring forth the fruit of good works.

—CHURCH OF ENGLAND

Stir up, we beseech thee, the pudding in the pot. And when we do get home tonight, we'll eat it up hot.

—CHOIRBOY PARODY

LUCKY CHARMS

The English also placed silver charms in the pudding to bring luck. A boot, bell, wishbone, thimble, ring, button, and horseshoe were popular choices. Some meanings have been lost, but in general, the boot predicted travel, the ring an impending marriage, the wishbone the granting of a wish, the thimble spinsterhood (ouch!), and the bachelor's button luck—for a man. Silver sixpences and threepenny bits were also put in puddings, signifying good fortune. Silver coins continued to be placed in puddings long after a family lost its little charms, but after World War II coins were made of copper and brass alloys, which reacted during the cooking process, so the tradition of placing little surprises to be found became rare.

HE WHO WEARS THE CROWN . . .

The Christian holiday Epiphany, also called Twelfth Night and/ or Three Kings Day, often includes a Twelfth Night Cake, also called a King Cake, honoring the three wise men who visited the baby Jesus on the twelfth day after his birth. However, this tradition actually predates Christian times. Ancient Romans served a similar item, and the cake, a basic yeast-based brioche filled with dried fruits and nuts, descends from ancient Arab recipes. The cake was popular throughout Europe in the Middle Ages, and as Europeans resettled in America they brought the tradition with them.

What the Bean Means . . .

While preparing the Twelfth Night Cake, the cook dropped a bean, coin, or other small object into the batter. If a man found the object in his slice of cake, he became King of the Bean. If a woman received the bean, she became queen and appointed a man as king. The king presided over the evening's entertainments and could command guests to do his bidding.

A Cake by Any Other Name . . .

Okay, they all mean "king's cake," but the varying names sound so exotic . . . or not:

Louisiana—king cake
France—*gâteau des rois*
Germany—*Dreikongskuchen*
Scotland—black bun
Portugal—*bolo rei*
Spain—*rosca de reyes*

Gâteau des Rois, Louisiana Style

Louisianans bake their king cake during the Louisiana carnival season, beginning in January and ending at Mardi Gras. They also include a red bean, sometimes covered in gold or silver leaf, or a figurine of the baby Jesus. Whoever gets the bean or figurine is considered lucky. Before the Civil War, American king cakes often contained gold or diamonds instead of beans; after the war, with the end of gala Creole balls in Louisiana, peas, beans, pecans, and coins were used, and in 1871 the tradition began that the queen of the Mardi Gras was determined by who found the prize in her cake. In 1872, the Rex Krewe, a Mardi Gras parade organization, chose to decorate its cake with purple, green, and gold icing, which came to have meaning as well.

> purple = justice
> green = faith
> gold = power

Pour on the Charm

In centuries past, items were placed into Twelfth Night Cake, and the fun was to see who had what in each slice of cake. The items included

> a bean for the king
> a pea for the queen
> a clove for the knave
> a twig for the fool
> a rag for the harlot

LITTLE JACK HORNER WAS NO DUMMY

Jack Horner was a steward to the Abbot of Glastonbury, who had to take a pie to King George VII as a present from the abbot. The pudding contained title deeds to twelve manors, sent to the King in the hope that he would not pull down Glastonbury Abbey. The King only received eleven deeds, hence the plum for Little Jack Horner who pocketed the twelfth deed.

Little Jack Horner
Sat in the corner,
Eating of Christmas pie:
He put in his thumb,
And pulled out a plum,
And said, "What a good boy am I!"

WHO DO WE HAVE TO BLAME FOR FRUITCAKE?

The fruitcake dates back to the thirteenth century, when dried fruits began to arrive in Britain from Portugal and the east Mediterranean. Early versions of the rich fruitcake, such as Scottish black bun, were luxuries for special occasions. In the early eighteenth century, bride cakes and plum cakes became cookery standards. Making a rich fruitcake in the eighteenth century was a major undertaking. Fruit was washed, dried, and pitted; sugar, cut from loaves, was pounded and sieved; butter was washed in water and rinsed in rosewater. Eggs were beaten for a half hour. Yeast, or barm from fermenting beer, had to be coaxed to life. Finally, the cook had to cope with wood-fired baking ovens that delivered uneven heat at best and occasionally flamed out before the cake was fully cooked.

FRUITCAKE *IS* FOREVER

Even though the *Guinness World Book of Records* doesn't include a category for the oldest known fruitcake, many tales are told of circulating fruitcakes that get passed around and around and around. . . . Here's one tale by humorist Russell Baker, from the December 25, 1983, issue of the *New York Times*:

> *Thirty-four years ago, I inherited the family fruitcake. . . . When my grandmother inherited it, it was already eighty-six years old, having been baked by her great-grandfather in 1794 as a Christmas gift for President George Washington. Washington sent it back with thanks, explaining that he thought it unseemly for Presidents to accept gifts weighing more than eighty pounds. . . . There is no doubt . . . about the fruitcake's great age. Sawing into it six Christmases ago, I came across a fragment of a 1794 newspaper with an account of the lynching of a real-estate speculator in New York City.*

A RUM A TUM TUM

When they were growing up in Pennsylvania, Susan and her sister Rozanne always picked at the fruitcakes their mother invariably bought, wondering aloud what on earth that pea-green thing was, or that squishy nut-like substance. The real mystery was why their mother bought the fruitcakes at all, as no one—not even their mother—ever ate an entire piece. At the end of the holiday season, they'd toss the remnants into the Allegheny River in what they liked to call their Saying Farewell to Christmas ritual.

When both Susan and Rozanne had graduated from college and moved to New York, they decided to create a new family tradition and bake their own fruitcakes. Rozanne was an earth mother at the time, baking her own bread, canning fruits and vegetables and pickles, so they searched for the perfect recipe, one that would make not only an edible, but a delicious, fruitcake. On the day they got together to mix up the cakes, to get them in the holiday mood they sipped cheap rum and Cokes. As they mixed the ingredients—consisting of identifiable fruits and nuts—every time they poured another rum and Coke, they would pour a little rum in the mix. They slaved for hours and hours, finally wrapping their creations in floured sacks and storing them in Rozanne's attic. Six weeks later, they wrapped each fruitcake in fanciful Saran wrap and shipped them off to their relatives—including their teetotaling grandmother who never drank alcohol—at all, ever. They got so carried away with the brilliance of their creation and how certain they were that everyone would love it that they forgot to keep one for themselves. They didn't get to sample even a taste.

When the reviews came in they were raves, straight across the board. It wasn't until their Uncle Bob called to tell them that his family had gotten tipsy after eating two small slices that they realized they might have overdone it on the rum.

Unfortunately, the next year Susan moved to Boston and that was the end of their Christmas fruitcakes, but for every year afterwards, until she passed, their Grandmother wrote them sweet letters around Thanksgiving with one request—Send me more of your famous fruitcake, please!

> ## Schlemeel, schlemazel, hasenfeffer incorporated
>
> In Germany, they favor gingerbread cookies, spice cookies called pfeffernüsse, and lebkuchen cookies and Christmas tree–shaped cakes called baumkuchen . . . and bratwurst.

THE EYES HAVE IT

In Scandinavia, families favor *lefse,* similar to a tortilla and made with potatoes. In centuries past women would travel from house to house, spending three or four days making up to a year's supply of *lefse* for the household. They would often work over an open fire and by lantern light well into the evening. The finished rounds were stacked in barrels. Rounds were also stored in kistes (sea chests) or steamer trunks for fishermen packing provisions for long sea voyages. Often, the shed where this baking took place was also the place where beer was made.

For Christmas, they make sweet *lefse* that takes two days to prepare. They begin by taking extra care when peeling the potatoes to remove all the eyes, as they believe any left behind will come back to haunt you. They then boil, mash, and rice the potatoes before combining them with flour, cream, butter, and sugar. The dough is pressed into loaf pans and chilled overnight. The next day, they slice the dough into very thin slices and use a *lefse* stick to drape one piece onto a lefse griddle, where it sizzles before being flipped and folded. They are served with lots of butter and sugar.

MEASURING SANTA'S, UM, BALLS

Maybe it's because their Christmas falls during summer down under, but whatever the reason, of course Australians have unique customs, like celebrating Christmas on the beach. Here's a saucy recipe that captures the Aussie sense of humor and, well, machismo. These sausage balls are tasty and a tad wicked.

Santa's Sausage Balls

1 pound hot sausage [whatever kind of sausage you prefer, as long as it's hot]
10 ounces grated cheddar cheese
1 cup diced onions
3 cups Bisquick

Mix all ingredients by hand in a large bowl and knead well. Shape into 1-inch balls. Place on a lightly greased sheet or pan and bake at 350 degrees F for 30 minutes.

Pass the Snails, s'il vous plaît

In France, Christmas dessert is bûche de Noël, *a sponge cake filled with butter cream and decorated like a Yule log. Other holiday delicacies include oysters and escargot.*

BEWITCHING BEANS

In Italy, the twelve-day Christmas celebration winds down on January 6. The night before, children leave their shoes outside to await the arrival of their "Christmas witch," La Befana, who will leave goodies in their shoes—provided they haven't offended her. On January 6, Italian mamas serve a *torta della Befana,* a cake in which a large bean is hidden. Whoever gets the piece with the bean—or bites down on the bean if they don't see it first—has a lucky year ahead. In some areas of Italy they serve lentils, often in combination with sausage (*zampone*), to attract good fortune all year. In other areas, a sweet bread or cake like a *panettone* or a *torciglione* is sliced and served to all as a symbol of hope and prosperity.

OOPS . . . GET POTTERY BARN ON THE LINE

In some regions of Mexico the Christmas cornucopia includes *buñuelos,* deep-fried anise-flavored cookies covered with syrup or sugar and served in pottery bowls. Guests gobble up the cookies and then throw the bowls hard against the ground. The more they shatter, the better your good luck.

SOUP-KITCHEN CHRISTMAS

One year in the 1990s, four months before Christmas, our friend Gretchen landed a job at a posh family-owned winery in the Napa Valley (that shall remain unnamed). As Christmas approached, everyone was buzzing about the company celebration. In expectation of a fancy repast, Gretchen hadn't eaten much the night before and nothing on the day of the party. Soon after the party got underway, in a barn on the property that had been gaily decorated with greenery (that would be moved to the owner's mansion afterwards), Gretchen noticed that the cheese and crackers being served lacked imagination—envision a very common sliced cheddar and saltines served on small plates. Next, everyone lined up for soup, and to Gretchen's great surprise, each was served a ladleful of soup sadly lacking in meat or flavor. "There was one miniature shrimp floating in broth, with a sprig of parsley," she revealed. After the soup bowls had been collected, Gretchen waited and waited and waited—through a ridiculous gift exchange that involved delivering a cheap useless gift and reciting an insulting toast (that the winery owner called an "amusing roast")—but neither plates nor a main course arrived. When the waiters brought out dessert, consisting of a small slice of vanilla cake with green frosting and two store-bought sugar cookies for each person, Gretchen turned to the person next to her. "Where's the main course?" she asked, adding, "I'm starving."

The person next to her snorted, stifling a belly laugh. "Oh, dearie," she said, "that's it. That's all we ever get."

To cap it off, the company announced that sales had dropped off slightly that year, so Christmas bonuses would be cut to $100 per person—another crushing blow to Gretchen, who had earmarked those funds for presents for her children. The capper came fifteen minutes later, when she overheard the grand dame of the winery ordering fresh guinea fowl from England to be flown overseas in time for her family's Christmas dinner.

By the next Christmas Gretchen had found another job, but she still often recounts the story of her soup-kitchen Christmas.

Hold Your Nose

In Greenland, the raw flesh of an auk (a penguin-like bird) is wrapped in seal skin and buried under a stone where it, uh, ripens for several months, until it's achieved what many might consider a dangerously advanced stage of decomposition. For the Greenlanders, this delicacy is a Christmas treat called Kiviak. Those who live to tell the tale say it smells like old blue cheese and tastes very pungent.

BRING ON DA OIL

Hanukkah marks the rededication of the Temple of Jerusalem after years of war and persecution. When the Holy Temple was regained, there was only a small amount of oil to light the menorah. Miraculously, it burned for eight days, until more oil arrived. Some ingenious soul linked the thankfulness for lamp oil with an appreciation of cooking oil—and latkes, potato pancakes fried in oil and served with applesauce and sour cream, have become the perfect Hanukkah delicacy. Apples and honey or gelt, chocolate "coins" wrapped in gold foil, are popular with the children. In Israel, many like to fry up doughnuts called *sufganiyot*.

LIQUID CHRISTMAS COURAGE

Christmas just wouldn't be Christmas without liquor, lots of liquor. We begin our best of the best weird alcohol traditions with something crafted with Hanukkah in mind.

Beer with Chutzpah

Mixing Torah references with pop culture references, Jeremy Cowan, owner of Shmaltz Brewing Company, created a line of "kosher" ales to celebrate Hanukkah. A jokester at heart, he dubbed the brand HE'BREW, the Chosen Beer, and peppered his products with catchy names like Genesis Ale, Messiah Bold, Jewbelation, and Rejewvenator. He launched the beer at a party dubbed Challahpalooza on Hanukkah 1996, after which he traveled for forty days and forty nights with cases of the "kosher" beer in his trunk, hawking his wares to liquor stores and bars, case by case. The creator calls his twenty-two-ounce bottled beers a celebration of hip Jewish culture. "It's all about the shtick," Cowan said.

On the labels, Cowan uses, well, shmaltz to sell his beer, inserting phrases such as "Exile never tasted so good" or "Don't pass out, Passover" or "Doppelbock . . . Shmoppelbock" or "Arise noble Rejewvenator." All the beer labels weave together religion, numerology, and humor and are entertaining to read. A video on his Web site begins with, "Two Jews walk into a bar . . ." and another video shows a young man who just graduated from medical school visiting his grandfather in a nursing home, where he is assailed by his grandfather's friends complaining about phlegm. The next frame shows the young man in a bar ordering HE'BREW, the Chosen Beer. The tagline reads, "Sometimes it's hard being Jewish, and sometimes it isn't."

All kidding aside, Cowan has spent more than a decade perfecting his brand to make it fun—and delicious. In an interview with the *Jewish Journal*, Cowan revealed that he "didn't want the beer to ruin the taste of the *varnishkes* to follow." Using what he calls "marketing as menschlekeit," Cowan touts the beer as "perfect for Bar Mitzvahs, weddings, and circumcisions."

Glogg, Glogg, Glogg

In Finland, Christmas wouldn't be Christmas without glogg. It's basically mulled wine, Finnish style—i.e., pour on the vodka, of course. Families typically have their own special ingredients.

Glogg

    1 bottle red wine
    2–3 tablespoons Madeira (optional, as in maybe a
        tad more won't hurt)
    ½ cup sugar or honey
    ⅓ cup raisins
    1 stick cinnamon
    5–6 whole cloves
    Thinly sliced peelings of 1 orange
    ¼ cup slivered almonds
    ¼ cup vodka (optional, as in how much is up to
        you!)

Combine all ingredients except vodka in a large pot and heat slowly until steaming hot. (Avoid boiling, since this will cook off the alcohol.) Add more sugar to taste. Before serving, add vodka, and then more vodka, and then . . . Serves 6.

Captain Rummy

According to reports by one of our hardiest early Americans, Captain John Smith, the first eggnog made in the United States was consumed in his 1607 Jamestown settlement. "Nog" comes from the word grog, which refers to any drink made with rum.

Top o' the Christmas Mornin' to You

No one toasts like the Irish, who will lift a pint and wish luck to you and everyone else on the planet—one person at a time. Here are a few Irish toasts to celebrate Christmas or to cheer in the new year:

> May you have food and raiment,
> a soft pillow for your head.
> May you be forty years in heaven
> before the devil knows you're dead.

> May you never be without a drop at Christmas.

> May your corn stand high as yourself,
> your fields grow bigger with rain,
> and the mare know its own way home
> on Christmas night.

> I wish you a Merry Christmas
> And a Happy New Year,
> A pocket full of money,
> And a cellar full of beer!

May your sheep all have lambs,
but not on Christmas night.

A Stroll Down Candy Cane Lane

Just in case you didn't know,
candy canes are an American
invention. A few fun facts
about candy canes:

For 200 years, the candy
cane came in only one color—
white.

National Candy Cane Day is
celebrated December 26 in the United States.

The world's largest candy cane was created by
Paul Ghinelli and measured 58 feet, 2¼ inches.

Each year 1.76 billion candy canes are made—
enough to stretch from Santa Claus, Indiana, to
North Pole, Alaska, and back again thirty-two
times—a whopping 96,000 miles!

PARTY LIKE IT'S 2099

New Year's Eve and New Year's Day parties always bring out the party people, and special foods usually grace the table. Let's take a trip across the globe to see how they celebrate in Japan.

The $10,000 Dinner

Of all the annual holidays in Japan, the New Year (*o-shogatsu*) is often spoken of as the "most Japanese" of celebrations. Dating back a thousand years, the traditional New Year's celebration is sprinkled with symbolism, expressed through food—and presentation. Because the Japanese believe that the first few days of the new year should be full of joy and low on stress, they spend days preparing *osechi ryori*, special food that is prepared only once a year, to provide meals for the first three or four days of the new year. The foods carry wishes for the new year and are artfully presented in a four-tier lacquer box called a *jubako*. The tradition began as a way for families to survive the first few days of the new year, when merchants shuttered their doors, and the food was designed to be able to last without refrigeration for four days.

Today most *osechi* is purchased, either at department stores or at local supermarkets. Prices can be exorbitant, topping off at the equivalent of $10,000! The luxury food is prepared by Japan's most famous chefs—or more likely, their most famous restaurants—and is limited in production. High-priced department stores like Takashimaya start taking orders for *osechi* in late October, and often the most popular varieties sell out within a few days.

Inside the decorated lacquer boxes, the food is arranged to achieve a balance of color and design. *Osechi* artisans will create ornate designs, representing seasonal shapes such as pine cones and plum flowers, or sea animals like octopus.

Eat Your Sardine Candy for a Good Harvest
Some of the foods the Japanese prepare are symbolic of their good wishes for the new year:

> *Kobumaki*—Kelp rolls (happiness)
> *Kuromame*—Simmered black beans (health)
> *Datemaki*—Rolled sweet omelet (knowledge)
> *Tazukuri*—Candied dried sardines (good harvest)
> *Kazunoko*—Herring roe (fertility)
> *Ebi-no-saka-mushi*—Sake-steamed shrimp (long life)
> *Pink and White Kamaboko*—Fish cakes (rising sun)
> *Tai-no-shio-yaki*—Grilled sea bream (for good fortune, joy)

When in Tokyo
If you ever find yourself in Japan for New Year's, you might try ringing in the new year by screwing your courage to the sticking pagoda and sampling

> *Kurikinton*—Mashed sweet potato with sweet chestnuts
> *Kinpira Gobo*—Braised burdock
> *Namasu*—Pickled daikon (radish) and carrot
> *Nimono*—Simmered vegetables, including gobo (burdock root), satoimo (taro), renkon (lotus root), carrots, shiitake mushrooms, and more

If you're really feeling brave, try tasting vinegar-seasoned octopus—squid, cucumber, grilled shrimp, and Japanese turnip in a marinade of vinegar and lemon juice. Marinated pond smelt is also popular. Many families also eat *mochi*, a rice cake prepared by pounding rice into a sticky dough.

What a Cutup

In China, they believe that holiday food must be prepared ahead of time to avoid the possibility that using a knife during New Year's might "cut luck."

EMANCIPATE ME

In America, some African Americans like to celebrate Kwanzaa, which is also called Emancipation Day or Jubilee Day. The tradition dates back to 1863 when the Emancipation Proclamation was read in Boston, announcing the release of slaves. Many African-American churches will hold "watch services" to commemorate the day, and often culminate the celebration with a feast of ham hocks, black-eyed peas, collard greens, and macaroni and cheese. For dessert, they serve sesame wafers (*benne* wafers) to represent the prospect of good fortune.

Bantu for You

The Bantu, who brought us benne *wafers, believe that sesame brings good luck. Benne means sesame in Bantu.*

Lucky Benne Wafers

These delicious African crispy sesame cookies are popular in the South—and a staple on Kwanzaa.

>1 cup toasted sesame seeds
>1 stick melted butter
>1½ cups brown sugar
>1 egg
>1 teaspoon vanilla extract
>1 cup all-purpose flour
>A pinch of salt
>¼ teaspoon baking powder

Preheat oven to 375 degrees.

Combine all ingredients in a large bowl; mix well.

Spoon cookie dough in coin-sized dollops onto a greased cookie sheet a minimum of two inches apart. Bake at 375 degrees for 5 minutes or until puffy and light brown on the edges. Cool on a wire rack and serve.

Note: You can toast your own sesame seeds by putting them in an oven at 350 degrees until they turn light brown—about 10 minutes. Makes 3 dozen.

Giving Thanks to Africa

Some of our favorite Southern foods come from Africa and are traditionally served on Kwanzaa, including

- Sweet potatoes
- Collard greens
- Okra
- Black-eyed peas
- Peanuts

EATING FOR LUCK

New Year's brings its own reason for celebration—saying good-bye to the old and ringing in the new has always included grand feasts and drinking, lots of drinking. For whatever reason—often no real reason—certain foods have become harbingers of luck.

In almost every culture, you'll find certain foods that people like to eat on New Year's and often believe will bring them luck. Step up to the buffet and give these a try.

You Lucky Pig, You

Pigs, whether a roasted suckling or ham hocks, are lucky all over the world. Some say pigs are portentous because they root themselves before walking forward, unlike those bottom-feeder lobsters that scurry backward. Some favor pork and pork products because they are extra fatty and will (logically?) fatten the family's purse. (Note: No one likes chicken for New Year's; chickens have to scratch the ground for their food.)

Pigs and Oranges

The Irish roast a pig and give oranges to the children for luck all around.

Lucky Pigs, Marzipan Style

Austrians decorate their table with miniature marzipan pigs. More lucky pigs!

The Pinker Your Pig, the Better Your Luck

Australians favor pink pig cookies for luck.

What Not to Eat

Avoid the aforementioned chicken or lobster, along with any winged fowl. In many Asian cultures eating birds at New Year's is considered dangerous, as they may fly away with your money.

Black-Eyed Pea Toss

Southerners favor black-eyed peas, because they are often shaped like coins, with ham hocks for that extra boost, and corn bread, because, um, it's *bread*. They also serve collard greens by the bushel because the more you eat, the richer you get.

Dialing for Donuts

People in Holland like to eat oily fried foods, and fry up dough-nuts stuffed with apples, raisins, and currants, because they're yummy.

Green Is for Lira

Italians prefer lentils, because they're also shaped like coins, and they're green—the color of money.

Put Your Best Foot Forward

In Scotland, where New Year's is called Hogmanay, they honor a tradition called "first footing," in which the first person to enter a home after the new year determines what kind of year the residents will have. If there are single women in the home, a handsome, dark-haired "first footer" of the male persuasion portends well for their marital prospects. First footers take their duty seriously and often bring symbolic gifts like coal, to keep the house warm, or baked goods—shortbread, oatcakes, and a fruitcake called black bun (with a surprise inside to bring luck to the guy or gal who snags it)—to make sure the household always has food.

Coddle Me

Supposedly cod became a sacred food because it was easily stored and transported and could travel safely from the Mediterranean to Africa and other distant ports. The Danish like it boiled, the Italians salted, and the Swedes cover all their bases by having it in a seafood salad.

Sauerkraut for Good Luck

Germans generally prefer sauerkraut—because it's a form of cabbage, a slang term for money in many cultures—with short ribs, which makes no sense at all, but hey, they taste better than ham hocks.

Biting the Head of the Herring

Some Americans, most particularly those of German or Polish descent, consider pickled herring their lucky talisman. They'll pickle the herring in brine and roll it around onions to create rollmops. To experience good luck in the new year, they must pop the rollmops into their mouths at the stroke of midnight. More adventurous families have been known to serve the pickled herring solo and to bite off the head of the herring at the stroke of midnight.

Peel Me a New Year's Grape

Spanish, Mexican, Cuban, and Portuguese families eat twelve grapes at the stroke of midnight, one for each month. The Peruvians like to add one more for extra good luck. And then, many like to wash it down with champagne.

No Sour Grapes

If the grapes you eat on New Year's are sour, then you're in for a bad year.

The Red, Red Pomegranate

The Turkish like pomegranates because the red color is lucky and the seeds look like coins.

The Lucky Almond

The Norwegians hide a whole almond in rice pudding. Surprise! It's good luck for the new year.

The Color of Kale

Because it's the color of money, the Danish eat steamed kale, sprinkled with sugar and cinnamon and smothered in a white sauce, for good fortune in the new year.

The Circle of Life

Eastern Europeans serve circle-shaped cookies to bring things full circle.

One for Me and One for Basil

In Greece, they bake a special round cake called *vasilopita*, in which they hide a coin. At midnight or after the New Year's Day meal, they cut the cake, offering the first piece to St. Basil before doling out the rest according to age.

Field of Dreams

The Japanese eat herring roe for fertility, shrimp for long life, and dried sardines for a good harvest—because sardines were once used to fertilize rice fields.

Swim with the Sharks

The Vietnamese like a glutinous rice cake filled with beans and ground meat and cooked in banana leaves, and shark-fin soup.

Invite Over the Richest Person You Know

Scots and Asians court good fortune when the first person to cross their threshold in the new year is someone happy, rich, and powerful. If you don't know anyone with all those stellar qualities, just settle for rich.

> ## *Wrap It Up*
>
> *To wish good fortune for their friends and family, Chinese families give money to each other in red envelopes.*

108th Time Is the Charm

The Buddhists munch on crunchy noodles at midnight (for long life)—and ring the monastery bells 108 times.

Heart as Black as Coal

On New Year's some Buddhists prepare and eat *guthok*, made of nine special ingredients, one of which is charcoal. If you're the unlucky soul who spoons up the charcoal, prepare to be ostracized, or maybe even thrown out of the temple, as you, my friend, have an evil heart.

START THE NEW YEAR CLEAN

In some Asian countries, families ready their houses and their lives for the new year by getting it shipshape. Since the first days will set the tone for the year, they scrub their houses, pay their debts, and purchase new clothes.

Hoppin' John

Some Southerners use black-eyed peas to make a dish they call Hoppin' John. Supposedly this tradition dates back to the Civil War, when the town of Vicksburg, Virginia, ran out of food while under attack and had to survive on black-eyed peas.

WHO WAS HOPPIN' JOHN?

When it comes to Hoppin' John, legends abound. Pick your favorite from the list below:

- Hoppin' John was a man named John who loved black-eyed peas so much he hopped with glee each time his long-suffering wife made them for dinner.

- In South Carolina, the local vernacular of old includes "Hop in, John," which was a way of asking someone over for dinner.

- Some say the phrase dates back to 1841, when this tasty black-eyed pea treat was sold on the street in Charleston, South Carolina, by a disabled African American called Hoppin' John.

Chapter Seven
PARTY HEARTY

How the Rest of the World Celebrates

All the world loves a party, and every culture finds unique ways to celebrate the holidays and ring in the new year. If you need proof, here's a list of the holidays, from beginning to end:

November 1	All Saints' Day
November 11	St. Martin's Day (Germany)
Last Thursday in November	Thanksgiving Day (USA)
Fourth Sunday before Christmas	Advent begins
December 6	St. Nicholas's Day
December 8	Bodhi Day in the Buddhist faith
December 10	Hanukkah begins (date varies)
December 13	Santa Lucia's Day (Italy, Sweden)
December 15–16	Posadas or Novena begins (Mexico)
December 17	Hanukkah ends (date varies)
December 19	St. Nicholas's Day (Julian calendar)
December 20	St. Ignatius's Day (Romania)
December 20/21	Winter Solstice
December 21	St. Thomas's Day
December 23	Little Christmas (Denmark)

December 24	Christmas Eve
December 25	Christmas Day
December 26	St. Stephen's Day
December 26	Boxing Day (England)
December 26	Kwanzaa begins
December 27	St. John's Day, Mother Night
December 28	Holy Innocents Day
December 30	Bringing in the Boar
December 31	New Year's Eve, St. Sylvester's Eve
December 31	Hogmanay (Scotland)
January 1	New Year's Day, St. Basil's Day
January 2	Snow Day, Holde's Day
January 3	Evergreen Day
January 4	St. Distaff's Day
January 5	Epiphany Eve
January 6	Epiphany, Three Kings Day, Twelfth Night
January 7	Russian Christmas
First Monday after Epiphany	Plough Monday (England)
January 13	Twentieth Day
January 13	St. Knut's Day (Scandanavia)

HOLIDAY SUPERSTITIONS

What would Christmas be without superstition? A trifle boring, one suspects. Many of the world's modern-day traditions stemmed from Celtic, druid, and pagan cultures, and many were incorporated into Christmas decorations used or foods served because it was believed that certain plants were evil and other plants had protective qualities. We're giving them to you in a list—pick and choose your favorites.

Beware the Evergreens

Since antiquity, all over the world, evergreens were used to spruce up houses throughout the winter holidays. Makes one wonder how something so beloved could also be a source of fear, but oh, dear friends, the mighty evergreen apparently packed a potent punch. Some superstitions included the following:

- Don't be so eager to celebrate. If you decorate before Christmas Eve, you'll attract evil spirits.

- Beware the negative vibes of ivy. Always pair it with holly—and be careful how you bring it into the house. If you bring the prickly holly in first, a man will rule your roost; if smooth ivy leads, the woman. For harmonious relations, join together with your spouse to bring in the smooth and the prickly parts at the same time.

- Holly wards off witches and lightning, but you have to treat it respectfully. Don't use it to clean your chimney or house.

- Place ivy leaves in a bowl of water on New Year's Eve and leave them soaking until Twelfth Night. If the ivy remains fresh and green, you'll have a good year ahead. If dark spots appear on the leaves, you could have really bad luck, become ill, or even die.

- Carefully collect all the evergreens and either burn all the greenery after the holidays, or feed them to the cows before Twelfth Night or Candlemas Eve (February 1). You have to diligently pick up every stray needle, as failure to do so could lead to the death of a family member. (Makes us think a mother dreamed this one up so her children would carefully sweep the hearth.)

- Make your own Yule logs and keep them burning all night on Christmas Eve—or throughout the Christmas holidays.

- Save a piece of the log for the next year's fire for luck.

- Never let a barefooted woman or a squinty-eyed man touch your Yule log.

Charming Superstitions

Every culture had its share of charming superstitions as well. Some of our favorites include these:

- Every time a man kissed a woman under the mistletoe, he had to pluck and give her one of its berries. Mistletoe held such charm that women would swipe sprigs from the church decorations and slip them into their pillowcases at night, hoping to dream about their future husband. Some would take the berry given to her after a kiss and a sprig from the mistletoe and sew it into her corset in hopes it would bind her to her suitor as long as the leaf lasted. Some would consider a berry from a man as a sign that he was ready to marry and give her a child.

- Young unmarried girls would cut a twig from a cherry tree on December 4 and place it in water. If the twig bloomed by Christmas Eve, she would be married within a year.

- If the first visitor on Christmas was a dark-haired man, you would have good fortune. If a red-haired man was the first visitor on New Year's Eve, that was a bad omen, as was a woman arriving first. The red-haired man could redeem himself if he blocked the woman from entering first. The gender of the first visitor to the house on

Christmas Eve was said to foretell the sex of the child of the pregnant women in the household.

- First footers—the first to arrive—should always bring evergreens or coals for the fire. If the first footer was a grown man, he would be offered food and drink; if he was a boy, he would be given a coin or two. First footers would make sure to kiss all the women in the house.

- The Irish believed that the gates of heaven open at midnight on Christmas Eve so anyone who dies around that time gets to go straight to heaven, whether they deserve to go to purgatory or not.

- In Germany, they would blindfold a goose and have girls circle it. The first girl to touch the goose would be the first to get married.

- The weather throughout the Twelve Days of Christmas portends the weather for each month of the new year, respectively.

- Nothing sown on Christmas Eve will perish, even if you plant it in the snow.

- Carols could only be sung during the Christmas holidays, and carolers must always be treated royally and given drink, food, or money.

- Wassailing occurred in the cow pastures, where farmers would honor their good fortune by lighting fires and drinking toasts to their crops, their fruit trees, and their livestock. While downing cider, they would fire off guns to scare away evil spirits. Some would place a plum pudding on a cow's horn. If it fell forward, they would have a good harvest; if it fell backward, not so good.

- In many European countries, they believed that anyone born on Christmas Day would be lucky, indeed. They wouldn't have to worry about ghosts or witches or evil spirits lurking at their door. Since they could rest assured that they would not die an untimely death, they could live an adventurous life. However, in other countries, a child born on Christmas Eve or Christmas Day could be unlucky. In Greece, the child might become a wandering spirit or Kallikantzaroi. In Poland, the child might become a werewolf!

Weird Superstitions

Oh by golly, there are weird superstitions galore. Feast on these!

- Candles had to be kept burning until they flamed out. If human shadows cast by the candlelight didn't have a head, that person would die within the year.

- A fir branch seared in a fire and then placed under your bed would protect you from lightning.

- You must fling open your doors at midnight on Christmas Eve so evil spirits will rush out into the cold night air. The next morning, the first person to open the door must shout, "Welcome, Old Father Christmas!" and then, sweep the threshold with a broom to brush away any remaining evil.

- Never launder a Christmas present before gifting it; doing so will wash away any good luck.

Food Superstitions

Even food could be treacherous during the holidays, and we're not talking calories or fat content. Sample these food precautions:

- Don't cut into a Christmas cake until Christmas Eve, and save part of it for Christmas Day.

- If you refuse mince pie, you'll have bad luck for a year.

- Eat all the mince pie you can—the more you eat, the better your luck—but never eat it Christmas Eve or later than Twelfth Night.

- Eat plum pudding sometime during the Christmas holidays or you'll have bad luck.

- Everyone in the family, including babies, has to take a turn stirring the pudding. Each has to stir the pot at least three times, making sure they can see the bottom of the pot with each stir. Unmarried girls who forget to stir the pudding won't get married the next year. Everyone should make a wish when they stir, but keep it a secret if they want it to come true. Silver coins, thimbles, and rings should be dropped into the pudding, representing luck, prosperity, and marriage respectively.

- "Dumb cakes" should be prepared at midnight on Christmas Eve. To use the cake for divination, the preparer had to remain silent (or "dumb") while mixing the ingredients and placing it on the hearthstone. The preparer would prick her initials into the top of the cake and walk backwards to her bedroom, where she would hopefully dream of her beloved. If she was lucky, his initials would appear on the cake the next morning, signifying that he would become her husband.

- A loaf of bread left on the table after Christmas Eve dinner meant you'd have plenty of bread in the coming year.
- Eat an apple at midnight on Christmas Eve, and you'll be healthy in the coming year.

Shoe Superstitions

Yes, friends, shoes definitely got in on the act.

- In Greece, they would burn old shoes during the Christmas season to prevent bad luck in the year ahead.
- In England, they believed that you had to give at least one pair of shoes to someone poor during your life to enjoy heaven, so shoes were often gifted to the poor during Christmas.
- Some believed that giving shoes to friends on Christmas would encourage them to walk away from you.
- Wearing new shoes on Christmas Day brought bad luck.

CALLING ALL GHOSTBUSTERS

In Northern Europe, winter solstice celebrations, called Jol (pronounced Yule), were so rife with spooks that they came closer to our modern-day Halloween than anything we recognize as Christmas. Celebrating Odin, the god of intoxicating drink and ecstasy, as well as the god of death, the celebrations amounted to a Feast of the Dead—what one might call the anti-birth feast. Along with villagers, spirits, devils, Odin, and his ultra-spooky nightriders showed up to party. In pagan days, long before Christianity, the villagers made a special beer for Odin that was often mentioned in medieval lore. They would fill the tables with fresh food and drink until they literally sagged,

Saving a Place for Great-Great-Great-Grandpa

On the morning of Christmas Day, people in Portugal have a traditional feast called consoda *with a twist: Not only does the family get together to eat, but so do all the long-lost, ahem, dead relatives. The living even set out the good china and load up plates with the full Christmas repast for the deceased.*

making sure plenty was left behind for the roaming Yuletide ghosts. They also lit bonfires to keep the ghosts and devils at bay—which led, of course, to the Yule log that still plays a featured role in many European Christmas traditions.

CAREFUL OR YULE BE SORRY

Europeans have long believed that the Yule log was magical—so magical that they kept it burning for at least twelve hours and in some regions for twelve days. When Christmas was over, they would often snap off a small piece of the Yule log to protect the household from witches. They would also gather and sprinkle the ashes over their fields in hopes they would increase fertility, or drop them into their wells in hopes it would purify and sweeten the water. They also used the ashes to create spells or charms. Some believed the ashes could keep their cattle safe from vermin or disease; others thought they could ward off thunderstorms or hailstorms. Some scholars linked the Yule log to an ancient Scandinavian fertility god, even implying that the large, single log represented the god's phallus and that it must burn for twelve days to honor the god.

Ancient Yule Traditions

In England, they would traipse off into the woods to chop down their Yule log and then employ the oxen to drag the monstrous limbs home. To make it festive, they would walk alongside and sing happy Christmas songs. Once home, they decorated the Yule log with evergreens and sprinkled it with grain or cider before setting it afire.

In Yugoslavia, they cut their Yule logs just before dawn on Christmas Eve and made sure they were carried into the house at twilight. They decorated their logs with flowers, colored silks, and gold trimmings, and sprinkled theirs with wine and an offering of grain.

In France, or at least some outer regions of France, fetching the Yule log was a family affair. Everyone would gather for the journey into the woods, singing songs as they walked, in

---

Rolling in the Hay

In some areas of Poland, they celebrate the new year by taking a hayride into the forest and lighting a bonfire to sizzle their sausages and bigos (a hunter's stew, consisting of any and all meats or fowl with sauerkraut).

---

hopes that their songs would attract blessings for their crops and flocks. In Provence, families observed a sacred ceremony that involved circling the house three times with the log, and then christening it with wine before lighting it.

THE LAND WHERE NEW YEAR'S COMES BEFORE CHRISTMAS

Desperate to stop the pagans from having any fun, the Roman Catholic Church in the fourth century changed the date of Christ's nativity from January 6 to December 25. They hoped to thwart a pagan feast dedicated to the birth of the sun. However, in Armenia they didn't bow to the mandate of the Roman Catholic Church. They retained the original January 6 date, which means that their Christmas comes after New Year's. Even after they became part of Russia, a nation that frowned on religious holidays and encouraged civil holidays, Armenian Christmas celebrations remained sedate and religious in nature, and their New Year's celebrations far more grand and far more fun.

Armenian families always exchange gifts on New Year's Eve and visit friends and relatives, feasting everywhere they go, including in their own homes every time someone comes to visit. Visiting hours start in the evening on New Year's Eve and last until midnight. After that, family parties last until 2:00 a.m., followed by more visiting, which continues for several days.

Food is abundant and fresh, and holiday tables are laden with dried fruits, nuts, and pomegranates.

CARPE DIEM

In Bulgaria, in celebration of the end of the fishing season, they hold a winter festival called Nikulden on December 6. Since their St. Nikolay is also considered the protector of sailors and fishermen, their sailors always take St. Nikolay icons onboard during fishing trips, while their wives place icons into the sea, praying to St. Nikolay to bring their husbands safely home. To honor St. Nikolay, on December 6, they offer the day's catch to the saint. As soon as they land, before bringing any fish home, fishermen eat the first fish caught. Since the carp is considered St. Nikolay's servant, their wives prepare a fish dish, called *ribnik,* by wrapping carp and rice in dough. *Ribnik* is baked in the oven, often accompanied by two special loaves of bread and must be brought to church for a special blessing. Then, back at home, after he wafts burning incense over the food, the host raises the bread high and breaks it in half, keeping one half and leaving the other on the table for St. Nikolay. The cross-shaped crown bone from the fish head is considered sacred. It is either buried as protection for the house or a grandmother will sew it into a child's cap to protect him or her from evil. Food is left out on the table all day for visiting neighbors and other guests, and the day ends with tales of St. Nikolay steering ships safely home.

JESUS IS A GEMINI?

Based on the appearance of the beckoning star that the Magi described (most likely the planets Venus and Jupiter forming a single "beacon of light" appearing suddenly in the night sky) and the computed positioning of stars and planets, modern scientists estimated the date of Jesus's birth to be June 17, 2 B.C. We have Pope Julius I to thank for proclaiming December 25 as the day Jesus was born. You see, in the fourth century those pesky pagans were celebrating the winter solstice and Saturnalia, and Pope Julius thought Christianizing the celebration would keep them in line (we suppose). Because these holidays occurred in the dark, cold winter, people would bring evergreens into the house to remind them that spring would come, eat fatty foods to warm their bodies, and use candles to shine light into their dreary winter lives. As such, these traditions became Christmas traditions, integral to the religious and familial celebrations. Of course one could easily say that customs such as bringing evergreens inside, eating fat-laden foods, and hanging lights are universal responses to the cold, dark winter season. Sometimes a doughnut is just a doughnut.

THE TWELVE DAYS OF HELL

According to Greek mythology, a gaggle of mythical bad boys called *Kallikantzaroi* creep out of the bowels of the earth to make their holidays a living nightmare. A cross between goblins

On a Dark and Spooky Night

Early Europeans believed in evil spirits, witches, ghosts, and trolls. As the winter solstice approached, with its long, cold nights and short days, many people were so afraid the sun would never return that they created special rituals and celebrations to welcome back the sun.

and spirits, these evildoers wreak havoc from Christmas Day to Epiphany. As with all mythical devils, descriptions of them vary from region to region. Some say they are dark, ugly, gigantic men suspiciously wearing iron clogs. Others describe them as short, swarthy creatures with cleft hooves, red eyes, monkey arms, and hairy bodies. Some describe them as lame, squinting, and stupid creatures who eat worms, frogs, and snakes.

Kallikantzaroi creep out during the Twelve Days of Christmas—at night, of course—and sneak into houses via the chimney, or sometimes right through the front door. Just to be safe, Greek families often keep a black-handled knife by their bed—the better to stab them with, one supposes. Others swear by hanging the lower jaw of a pig behind the front door or inside the chimney. Others try an assortment of tactics. To keep them at bay,

- Hang a tangled strand of flax on the front door and they'll screech to a halt to tediously count the threads. If you're lucky, sunrise will frighten them back into their holes before they finish the task.

- Put more logs on the fire. Kallikantzaroi don't like sliding down smoke-filled chimneys. Booster effect: Toss in a thorny log in case one slips down anyway.

- Burn old shoes. The smell will knock them over, and if that doesn't work, toss salt onto the fire. They don't like strong smells or a crackling fire.

- Keep a sprig of basil handy. As long as someone dips the basil in water and sprinkles the entire house with it, they can ward off those nasty gremlins. If that doesn't work, when the priest blesses the water on Epiphany, he'll scare them back to their holes.

Garlic to the Rescue

Some Greeks still believe that a baby born on December 25 may be a demon child hell-bent on upstaging the Christ child. To ward off any chance of their child joining the ranks of the Kallikantzaroi, mothers will wrap strings of garlic around the infant.

- Scatter pancakes on your roof. Cyprus villagers toss sweet pancakes on their roofs to send their unwelcome visitors home happy.

WHO'LL STOP THE WREN

Irish folklore is rife with symbolism. Would you believe they celebrate December 26 as Wren Day? That's right, wren, as in birds. And they don't honor them—in fact, in the olden days, they would hunt those suckers down and kill them. Why? Legend has it that long ago, when the original Irish natives attempted to ambush Viking invaders, wrens beat their wings against the Viking shields, awakening them in time to fight. On another occasion, the Irish natives were launching an attack on their archenemies, a platoon of British soldiers, when, once again, those party-pooper wrens pecked on the drums of the snoozing soldiers and spoiled the battle. Unfortunately for the wrens, the Irish really know how to hold a grudge. Every December 26, they suit up and travel in processions from door to door luring their neighbors to join the hunt. They still blacken their faces with soot, and down a whole lotta pints, but they don't actually shoot wrens anymore (or at least that's what they tell us).

I SEE DEAD PEOPLE IN THE SAUNA

For Finns, the sauna is the sacred center of family life, where babies are born and the sick are healed and the dead come back for a little R&R every Yuletide. Every Christmas Eve afternoon, happy Finns everywhere heat up the family sauna for a long, sweaty soak with their dearly departed ancestors. As the sun slowly sets over the fjords, the spirits of the deceased return to the homeland sauna for some quiet quality time with the family before the hectic holiday officially begins.

Afterward, families often go to church and then to the cemetery, where they light candles on the graves of their deceased loved ones so that they can use the glow of the twinkling lights in the darkening evening to find their way back to their eternal sleep.

It's enough to make you sweat.

WHOA, NELLIE

In some rural areas of south Wales at Christmastime, and particularly on New Year's Eve, a person hiding under a horsehair sheet (a brethyn rhawn) impersonates the Mari Llwyd, a mythical grey mare, by positioning a horse's skull, with a hinged jaw and fiery (fake) eyes in the sockets, on a long stick. Often they drape the stick with white sheets and dangling ribbons or cowbells. In the old days, villagers would bolt their doors and windows when the Mari Llywds approached, and not relent until the mummers *riding the mare* would beg for food and drink. But first, the hungry mummers had to win a contest of wits, dubbed *pwnco.* Basically both sides traded insults, albeit rhymed Welsh insults. Eventually, a winner was declared, and the villagers would open the windows and doors and reward the mummers by offering them spiced warm beer, cake, and money, of course. The tradition had faded away in the early part of the twentieth century, but has made a slight comeback in recent years. Today, the celebrants may sing, but rarely attempt rhyming insults. Mostly the celebrants try to snap the Mari Llwyd's jaws open and nip arms or legs or fingers or whatever the old bitty can catch. Luckily, this horse's bite doesn't lead to an emergency room visit. In this case, if the Mari Llwyd nips you, the worst fate you'll encounter is an old-fashioned cash fine.

HAVE YOURSELF A ROMANTIC CHRISTMAS, JAPANESE STYLE

Just because there aren't many Christians in Japan, it doesn't keep the Japanese from celebrating Christmas in their own way. Only 1 percent of the population is Christian, so what they lack in suitable religious fervor they make up in food and ambiance. For the majority of the Japanese people, Christmas is celebrated as a secular holiday full of sex and romance—a sort of Santa Claus Does Valentine's Day. Indeed, they've even christened this holiday Romanchikku Kurisumasu (Romantic Christmas). Rather than going to Midnight Mass, amorous Japanese couples plan romantic dinners for two on Christmas Eve; many also indulge in an overnight stay in a sexy suite at a swank hotel. For dessert, they feed each other cute, semi-expensive Christmas cakes—typically sponge cakes decorated with whipped cream frosting and large, whole, upturned strawberries that protrude from the cream next to pudgy Santa figurines—the perfect Christmas date finger food.

KENTUCKY FRIED CHRISTMAS

There's no roasting a turkey in the small toaster ovens or stoves found in most Japanese kitchens, so they do the next best thing—they go out for their bird. In fact, on Christmas Day they pig out on—of all things—Kentucky Fried Chicken. Kentucki Furaido Kurisumasu, or "Kentucky Fried Christmas," began as a marketing ploy by KFC in the 1970s, and, weirdly enough, caught on. Leading up to Christmas, commercials depict grinning children munching happily on crispy drumsticks. Since Japan also doesn't have drive-thru restaurants, families make reservations in advance for "Kentucki" and will line up around the block to pick up their orders of Christmas Chicken.

Don't Light It Up

The small number of Christians in China celebrate Sheng Dan Jieh, which means Holy Birth Festival. Like Christians almost everywhere, they decorate their homes with evergreens, and a "tree of light" that they adorn with lanterns, flowers, and red paper chains that symbolize happiness.

MAKE MINE KINGS!

In Spain, many still focus on the religious aspect of Christmas. Rather than adopting the tradition of exchanging gifts on December 24 or 25, they bestow gifts on January 6, which they call Three Kings Day. On January 5, children go to a parade welcoming the three kings, who receive requests for presents. Later, before going to bed, children leave their shoes out in a visible spot in the house or on their balcony, in hopes that Mechior, Gaspar, and Balthasar will bring them their desired treasures. For breakfast or after lunch, families often have the typical dessert of the day, the *rosca de reyes*, a large ring-shaped cake that is decorated with candied fruits, symbolic of the emeralds and rubies that adorned the robes of the three kings. Somewhere inside the cake there is a surprise, and the person to find it will be crowned king or queen of the house for the remainder of the day.

THE POOP IN SPAIN STAYS MAINLY . . . IN THE FIREPLACE?

In the Catalan region of Spain, families toss a little something extra in their Christmas fires, something we find just a tad odd. It's called Tió de Nadal or *caga tió*, which loosely translates (pardon the pun) to a "pooping log." Families either hollow out their own log or buy one that is already hollowed out. They attach thick branches as legs, carve or paint a smiling face with a dimensional nose on it, and top it with a *barretina*, or red sock hat. Beginning on the first night of the Feast of Immaculate Conception, December 8, and throughout the holiday season, the family "feeds" the log bits of food, such as candies, nuts, and dry figs. On Christmas Eve or Christmas Day, they put their *caga tió* in the fireplace and, before torching it, gather around to sing a, well, pooping song—one that urges it to poop well or expect them to beat the poop out of him. If their little friend doesn't poop out all the food they've stuffed into him, they gleefully beat him with sticks until he poops out small candies, fruits, and nuts. When he is through, the final object dropped is a salt herring, a garlic bulb, or an onion. The poop is offered to friends and family as gifts, and the poor caga tió is set ablaze.

Catalonians also hide a little statue in their nativity scenes. As strange as it sounds, amidst displays of the entire town of Bethlehem and the blessed Mary and Joseph admiring the manger one will often find a *caganer*, or little pooping man, tucked away in a corner. Although no one seems to know why or how this began (perhaps as a plea for fertile fields or to remind people that Jesus was a human being, with normal human functions), this strange custom dates back to the seventeenth century and continues to be so popular that Catalonians now buy *caganers* resembling their favorite celebrities. Imagine their embarrassment at being caught with their pants down!

And Your Name Is?

Hong Kong celebrates Ta Chiu, a festival of peace and renewal, by making offerings to saints and reading the names of everyone who lives in the area.

IN SPAIN IT MAINLY RAINS . . . ON DECEMBER 22

In Spain, December 22 is a day when good fortune reigns. That's the day they announce the winning number of the famous Christmas Lottery. This lottery is a tradition dating back to 1763, when Carlos III initiated it. Since then, not one year has passed without it, and it has become the symbolic moment in which Spaniards begin to celebrate the Christmas holidays. Ticket vendors can be found in each of the metro entrances, on the streets, and in most stores. As a holiday promotion, stores offer complimentary lottery tickets to customers who spend over a fixed amount of money.

IT'S ONLY A PAPER CLOCK

Fed up with the commercialization of Christmas, in 1993 an organization called Same Sky in Brighton, England, orchestrated an event they dubbed Burning the Clocks as a secular celebration of the winter solstice. Participants created elaborate, fantastical paper and willow lanterns in the forms of clocks of all shapes and sizes, which they lit and carried in a parade to the beach. Drumming and music accompanied the marchers through the streets to the beach, where all the lanterns were placed in a pile and burned. The celebrations were capped off with fireworks and jubilation to welcome the lengthening of days. In recent years, the event has attracted over a thousand lantern-bearers and up to 20,000 spectators. As it has caught on, the designs have become even more artistic and fantastical . . . but they still burn the lanterns.

Quick Hits

Just for kicks, here's a short list of unique celebrations in exotic places:

- *In Italy, they fast for twenty-four hours before Christmas Eve so they can fully enjoy a celebration meal. Presents and empty boxes are drawn from the Urn of Fate, which always contains at least one gift for everyone. At twilight, they light candles and recite prayers and poems.*

- *In New Orleans, an ox decorated with holly and ribbons is paraded through the streets.*

- *In Alaska, a pole with a star is carried from house to house, followed by Herod's men, who try to capture the star.*

- *In Arizona, Mexican Americans often honor Las Posadas, a ritual procession and play representing Mary and Joseph's search for lodging by traveling to their neighbors' houses and having a look into each family's crib.*

- *In Hawaii, a Christmas tree ship arrives to herald the beginning of the Christmas season.*

SURF'S UP!

In Australia, Christmas Day can be hot, hot, hot. So these "islanders" often share their Christmas repast on the beach. We're told Bondi Beach in Sydney's eastern suburbs is often packed with picnickers, sharing turkey, ham, pork, and flaming plum puddings. On Christmas Eve they gather by the thousands to sing carols, and on Christmas Day Santa is likely to arrive via the sea—on a surfboard.

GET YOUR SKATE ON

Throughout the Christmas season, Venezuelans daily attend an early-morning church service called *Misa de Aguinaldo* (Early Morning Mass). In the capital city of Caracas, they will set off firecrackers and ring the church bells to rally worshippers out of their warm beds and into the predawn hours. Many neighborhoods block the streets so that its citizens can roller skate to church. Just for fun, right before bedtime children will tie one end of a piece of string to their big toe and hang the other out the window. The next morning, roller skaters give a tug to any string they see hanging. This goes on until *Nochebuena*, better known as December 24, when the last morning mass occurs. Families attend a mass on this night and then return home to a huge and fancy dinner.

THE WHITE MOON OF MONGOLIA

In Mongolia, the first new moon kicks off the new lunar year every February. This White Moon, called *Tsagaan Sar*, marks the start of a month-long celebration of travel, family, and food for the nomadic people. Given the far-flung population, this means that family members have to hit the road, traveling long distances across frozen deserts to visit their relatives.

When people travel so far to see you, it's only right that you feed and entertain them. The Mongolian women get busy early, spending weeks preparing 2,000–3,000 mutton dumplings (*buuz*), which they store outside in the cold freeze until the guests' arrival is imminent—and then they bring the *buuz* in and steam them.

Step into My Web

An artificial spider and web are often included in the decorations on Ukrainian Christmas trees. A spider web found on Christmas morning is believed to bring good luck.

Once the guests arrive, a veritable feast awaits them: steamed *buuz*, biscuits, and the boiled hindquarters of a sheep. For dessert they offer the traditional *booy* or "shoe-sole cake," a stacked cake of hard bread, curd, and sweets in an odd number of layers that have been shaped into long ovals and stamped to resemble shoe soles. Beverages include *airag* (fermented mare's milk, often called "white beer"), vodka, and tea with milk.

After their long trek across the desert, guests are usually happy to oblige the Mongolian custom of partaking in all the dishes served at dinner. (Not to do so would be considered an insult.) These feasts typically last late into the night. And as well they should—for they'll need plenty of *buuz* fuel to continue from hut to hut across the Mogoian desert to visit other friends and relations.

Are You Easy?

Over the White Moon holiday, relatives, neighbors, and friends come to visit. When they arrive, they greet each other by extending their hands, layering their palms face-up, and inquiring, "Amar bain uu?" which literally means, "Are you easy?" Friends and relatives use the occasion to show off their handcrafted deels, *the traditional long "Genghis Khan" coats, hats, and boots they have made or acquired over the past year.*

GETTING A JUMP ON THE PARTY CIRCUIT

In India, they celebrate their lunar new year, Diwali, in October or November. Diwali celebrations include a five-day festival of lights that varies according to the colorful regional myths behind the celebration:

Lord Krishna vs. Narkasur: Lord Krishna defeats the demon Narkasur.

Lord Rama vs. Ravana: Lord Rama defeats the demon Ravana.

Lord Krishna Morphs into a Dwarf: Lord Krishna transforms himself into a dwarf to dethrone an evil king.

The tales and the celebrations all have one thing in common—good triumphs over evil, and everyone parties afterwards. Betel leaves, betel nuts, plantains, fruits, flowers, and

---

Clean Enough for a Goddess

The day before Diwali, houses are cleaned and decorated, ovens are cleaned and smeared with lime. This is important, because it is said that Lakshmi, the goddess of wealth and prosperity, will only visit houses that are clean and brightly lit.

turmeric powder are set out. Children are anointed with oil and bathe at dawn to avoid unpleasant reincarnations, and receive new clothes and treats. During Diwali, they light small oil lamps to create flame designs around their houses and decorate their doors with richly colored *rangoli* (sand painting) patterns. Celebrations include spectacular light and fireworks displays.

There is no set dinner menu (though vegetarian curries are common), but neighbors traditionally exchange colorful sweets called *mithai,* made from semolina, wheat flour, chickpea flour (or thick milk with coconut), carrots or pumpkin, and spiced with cardamom and nutmeg.

Gambling usually follows dinner. Because the goddess Parvati played dice with her husband Lord Shiva on Diwali and decreed that those who gamble on this night will prosper throughout the year, everyone gambles with a clear conscience. Firecrackers and sparklers blaze and pop while families gather to eat and play cards.

Clean Sweep

In Norway on Christmas Eve, all the brooms in the house are hidden. This is because long ago it was believed that witches and mischievous spirits came out on Christmas Eve and would steal their brooms for riding.

GONNA WASH THAT SPOOK RIGHT OUTTA MY HAIR

In Japan, New Year's Eve is observed by thorough house cleaning, to rid the house of evil spirits before the new year begins. Bamboo sticks—symbols of growth and prosperity—are hung on the front door. At midnight, chimes ring 108 times, and children are given their New Year's money for good behavior during the year. The real celebration does not begin until sunrise, when the traditional meal of vegetables, seafood, and dessert is served in one dish—the different types of food symbolizing prosperity. The day after New Year's is First Writing Day, when *kakizome,* or the practice of writing down one's hopes for the year, is observed.

PICK ME!

In Mexico, the Christmas celebration of Posadas culminates on January 6 with the Fiesta de los Reyes, or Feast of the Kings. Naturally, King's Cake (*rosca de reyes*) plays a starring role. First, the yummy dough is shaped into a ring to symbolize a crown, and a teeny-tiny doll is folded into the dough. When the cake is served, the person who finds the doll on his or her plate becomes the king for the day and must select a queen. The "royal" couple has a twenty-six-day shelf life. Their final act as royalty is to host a party on Candlemas (February 2), when they light candles for the Virgin Mary.

Bucket Run

Long ago in Scotland, many observed a tradition called Creaming of the Well. At the break of dawn, single young women would make a mad dash for the well so they could snag the first water drawn for the day. If that woman could then trick the object of her affections into drinking said collected water, the fellow would marry her by the end of the new year.

Sources

http://www.petergreenberg.com
http://www.foodtimeline.org/christmasfood.html